# WE CAN BECOME PERFECT

## The Lord Has Prepared
## The Way

by

A. Harold Goodman

Max L. Waters

Published and Distributed by:

Granite Publishing and Distribution, LLC
868 North 1430 West
Orem, UT 84057
(801) 229-9023

ISBN: 1-890558-97-4

Library of Congress Catalog Card Number: 00-105815
Printed in the United States of America

Typeset by The Office Connection – Provo, Utah

Salt Lake Temple Spires by Eldon K Linschoten
© by Intellectual Reserve, Inc.
Used by Permission

# Introduction

Discovering and living the Gospel of Jesus Christ is an exciting experience, and nothing in this life is more rewarding or can bring greater joy to the individual. Oftentimes, though, the challenge of living a life patterned after our Master seems too awesome. Without the benefit of our pre-mortal understandings, we have a tendency of feeling we cannot reach perfection because of our weaknesses.

This book has been inspired from experiences and understandings that will help each person who reads it prayerfully to know more clearly who he is and that he can become perfect. As we begin this mortal life with all our weaknesses and constantly struggle to overcome the carnal and physical elements of this life, it is important to know we can learn to let the spirit reign. This is because of the atoning sacrifice of the Savior and the miraculous principle of repentance.

The authors have witnessed many changes in lives of others as the doctrines of salvation have been understood and lived. Please pray that the Holy Spirit will carry the intended message of encouragement and inspiration into your heart. It is our hope that as you read this book and ponder the scriptures that have been cited, you will more fully recognize that *We Can Become Perfect* because the Lord has prepared the way.

CHAPTER ONE

# Beginning the Way

Far too many of our Father's children look at the commandment to become perfect, "even as your Father which is in Heaven is perfect"[1] and say, "What's the use, I can't make it." Others try hard, but may become discouraged because they fail to realize that perfection is a life-long pursuit. It was never intended that we see our earthly mission as such a hopeless endeavor. But, because the vision of our full potential is often seen only dimly and sometimes too infrequently, an abiding faith and hope in Christ does not fully mature within us. Nothing pleases the adversary more than to blind the minds of our understanding so that we cannot feel the beginning of everlasting joy, or see the glory that lies ahead.

Although the sequence of experiences which enlighten the mortal soul and lead it back to the Father are different for each person, there are some eternal principles and commonalities about life which have not changed over the ages. There are some things that we can absolutely count on as guidelines. As Jesus taught, none of us receives a fullness of His doctrine, power or glory at first, but must continue from grace to grace until a fullness is received. We are judged by the light of knowledge we have been given and are promised even greater light and knowledge with accomp-

---

[1] Matthew 5:48.

1

anying laws to live as we experience the narrowing in process.

But in order to have the faith and the courage to "press forward" until we have obtained all that we are heirs to, we must know in our hearts that God loves us beyond our mortal ability to comprehend. He is long-suffering and kind. Tenderly He calls us by the voice of His spirit and desires that we each have full opportunity to perfect the mind, control the body and enlarge the soul, that we might become partakers of His divine nature to a certain degree here and fully in eternity. He is keenly aware of our every joy and our every sorrow. There is no thought or action which goes unnoticed or unrecorded. Careful plans have been laid whereby, through our obedience and faithfulness, we may lay hold upon every blessing promised the faithful, even all that the Father hath.[2]

## Nature of Perfection

We must obtain the assurance through humble prayer that he who stands at the helm will safely guide us through even the roughest storms of life. Perfection is not required or attainable at first, but as you become perfect, your life, mission and potential glory will be unfolded unto you. But first, you must know who you are and assess carefully your strengths and weaknesses, then proceed to inquire of the Lord to find your foreordination. The Lord declared to Moroni that he gives men weaknesses that they may be humble.[3] Our weaknesses were given us by the Lord with a promise that if we humble ourselves before Him, then will He make weak things become strong unto us. A vital factor to remember is that all mortals have weaknesses and strengths.

Many of the Lord's children have difficulty recognizing the tremendous potential they have mainly because of impediments that some way or other distort their vision. One such example was a sister who was a sophomore at college and had great problems preying upon her. She had indulged in serious sin. This guilt weighted so heavily upon her that there seemed to be no light or happiness in her life. Her countenance was depressively downcast. She seemed to be continually discouraged and expressed no hope

---

[2] See D&C 84:38.
[3] See Ether 12:26-27.

for the future.

After many months of striving to determine what problems were preying upon this girl's mind, her bishop, representing the Lord's church, encouraged her to pour out the magnitude of her burden to him. After several heart-rending hours of experiencing what it meant to have a broken heart and a contrite spirit, this young sister began to understand her eternal potential and to comprehend the glorious principle of complete repentance. In a few short months this sister started a completely new life. She radiated a wholesome attitude and her countenance began to glow with a deep concern for others, she saw a future that was limitless. Later she became president of the Relief Society in her ward and exerted tremendous leadership in the lives of all the sisters. In fact, her exciting goal was to have each of the 144 sisters active in Relief Society, and she achieved this goal before the year's end. What a miraculous change. Unfortunately, too many fail to find or to achieve this inner harmony.

## The Nature of Mankind

Doesn't it seem at times that you are almost two people? We are moved upon by the Spirit, and while under its influence deep spiritual feelings are felt. Some may have had moving spiritual experiences where there was such an outpouring of the spirit that they have spontaneously exclaimed within themselves, "Father, I love Thee, I desire all that has been prophesied by the Holy Prophets from the beginning even unto our time to be answered upon my head. I will never do this, or that, ever again!" Then twenty-four hours later find themselves back doing all the old things which they promised never to do again.

At such times it seems that the body and spirit cannot get together. Usually the spirit is willing, but as is often quoted, the body doesn't measure up. Paul apparently had some of these same struggles in getting his body to respond to the will of the spirit, for he wrote:

> *For that which I do I allow not: for what I would,*
> *that do I not; but what I hate, that do I . . . Now then it*
> *is no more I that do it, but sin that dwelleth in me.*
>
> *For I know that in me (that is, in my flesh,)*

> *dwelleth no good thing: for to will is present with me;*
> *but how to perform that which is good I find not.*
>
> *For the good that I would I do not: but the evil*
> *which I would not, that I do.*
>
> *Now if I do that I would not, it is no more I that do*
> *it, but sin that dwelleth in me.*
>
> *I find then a law, that, when I would do good, evil*
> *is present with me . . .*
>
> *But I see another law in my members, warring*
> *against the law of my mind, and bringing me into*
> *captivity to the law of sin which is in my members.*[4]

Not only do we contend with unrefined elements in an attempt to purify the body, but we also find that the disposition of the body is not naturally to yield to the teachings of its creator. Except the Lord worketh with our hearts to stir us up to a remembrance of Him, we do not easily keep our eyes focused upon how we might become perfect. These same tendencies and human frailties were observed by Nephi, the son of Helaman, among his people.

> *And thus we see that except the Lord doth chasten*
> *his people with many afflictions, yea, except he doth*
> *visit them with death and with terror, and with famine*
> *and with all manner of pestilence, they will not*
> *remember him.*
>
> *O how foolish, and how vain, and how evil, and*
> *devilish, and how quick to do iniquity, and how slow to*
> *do good, are the children of men; yea, how quick to*
> *hearken unto the words of the evil one, and to set their*
> *hearts upon the vain things of the world!*
>
> *Yea, how quick to be lifted up in pride; yea, how*
> *quick to boast, and do all manner of that which is*
> *iniquity; and how slow are they to remember the Lord*
> *their God, and to give ear unto his counsels, yea, how*

---

[4] Romans 7:15, 17-21, 23.

*slow to walk in wisdom's paths!*

*Behold, they do not desire that the Lord their God, who hath created them, should rule and reign over them; notwithstanding his great goodness and his mercy towards them, they do set at naught his counsels, and they will not that he should be their guide.*

*O how great is the nothingness of the children of men; yea, even they are less than the dust of the earth.*

*For behold, the dust of the earth moveth hither and thither, to the dividing asunder, at the command of our great and everlasting God.*[5]

Of all the creations, only man has turned his ear from and is disobedient to the commandments of his Creator. For this, only God's children can become devils. And sadly the author of this disobedience is reaping an awful harvest because of the hardness of men's hearts. Concerning this tendency in man, King Benjamin declared:

*For the natural man is an enemy to God, and has been from the fall of Adam, and will be, forever and ever, unless he yields to the enticings of the Holy Spirit, and putteth off the natural man and becometh a saint through the atonement of Christ the Lord, and becometh as a child, submissive, meek, humble, patient, full of love, willing to submit to all things which the Lord seeth fit to inflict upon him, even as a child doth submit to his father.*[6]

## The Potential of Mankind

In spite of these inherent weaknesses in mortality, we should keep clearly in mind the great potential for good that is in each person. Brigham Young taught that the devil does not have rule over both the body and the spirit. He said:

---

[5] Helaman 12:3-8.
[6] Mosiah 3:19.

> *I want to tell you that he does not hold any power over man, only so far as the body overcomes the spirit that is in a man, though yielding of the spirit of evil . . . The spirit is pure, and under the special control and influence of the Lord, but the body is of the earth, and is subject to the power of the devil, and is under the mighty influence of that fallen nature that is of the earth. If the spirit yields to the body, the devil then has power to overcome both the body and the spirit of that man, and he loses both. . . . When you are full of evil passion, and wish to yield to it, then stop and let the Spirit, which God has put into your tabernacles, take the lead. If you do that, I will promise you will overcome all evil, and obtain eternal lives. But many, very many, let the spirit yield to the body, and are overcome and destroyed. The influence of the enemy has power over all such. Those who overcome every passion, and every evil, will be sanctified, and be prepared to enjoy eternity with the blessed . . . But let the body rise up with its passions, with the fallen nature pertaining to it, and let the spirit yield to it, your destruction is sure.*[7]

The body will do only what you allow. It is within your power to resist the tempting adversary, to overcome all evil, and to claim the eternal blessings which are yours by birthright. Paul, after expressing concern about the natural tendencies of his body went on to instruct us regarding what we could do to claim our inheritance.

> *For if ye live after the flesh, ye shall die: but if ye through the Spirit do mortify the deeds of the body, ye shall live.*
>
> *For as many as are led by the Spirit of God, they are the sons of God.*
>
> *For ye have not received the spirit of bondage*

---

[7] Journal of Discourses 2:255-256.

*again to fear; but ye have received the spirit of adoption, . . .*

*The spirit itself beareth witness with our spirit, that we are the children of God:*

*And if children, then heirs; heirs of God, and joint-heirs with Christ; if so be that we suffer with him, that we may be also glorified together.*

*For I reckon that the sufferings of this present time are not worthy to be compared with the glory which shall be revealed in us.*

*For the earnest expectation of the creature waiteth for the manifestation of the sons of God.*[8]

The Lord pointed out to Joseph Smith some of the changes, promises and blessings which come after one has overcome all things. These rewards are reserved for those:

*. . . Who overcome by faith, and are sealed by the Holy Spirit of promise, which the Father sheds forth upon all those who are just and true.*

*They are they who are the church of the Firstborn.*

*They are they into whose hands the Father has given all things—*

*They are they who are priests and kings, who have received of his fulness, and of his glory;*

*And are priests of the Most High, after the order of Melchizedek, which was after the order of Enoch, which was after the order of the Only Begotten Son.*

*Wherefore, as it is written, they are gods, even the sons of God—*

*Wherefore, all things are theirs, whether life or death, or things present, or things to come, all are*

---

[8] Romans 8:13-19.

*theirs and they are Christ's, and Christ is God's.*[9]

According to the promises made with our forefathers, we can be like Him, think His thoughts, and obtain the power through faithful obedience to do the things He does.

## The Kingdom Is Within You

Where should I begin? Sooner or later each soul makes a conscious choice about certain priorities in life. These have been listed as the family, the Church, and one's vocation—in that order. But careful analysis suggests another dimension. You! It is utterly impossible for you to work out the salvation for a soul other than your own. When you marry you will find yourself growing together with your companion, but even then the challenging process of overcoming all things is an individual matter.

The Lord knows how and what will chasten each of His children who will hearken unto His voice. You then are the most important single individual in the plan. You indeed count!

Too frequently, though, this concern for self is misinterpreted as being egotistical. It is coming to know yourself and clearly identifying the talents you possess. When Jesus said, "behold, the Kingdom of God is within you,"[10] He meant it. You represent a potential for creating millions of worlds and begetting billions of spirit children, to whom in a very real sense, our heavenly Father becomes the grandfather. It is no wonder that He is both excited and concerned about each of us and what we are doing with our lives. Our success extends His work and His glory. There is no joy in heaven when any soul slips below his potential. Oh, if you could only see for a moment the organization of beings just beyond your sight who watch after you.

What about you? You are a child of God—called before ever the world was. Assigned to come through a noble heritage.

---

[9] D&C 76:53-59.
[10] Luke 17:21.

## The Lord's Invitation

Over the years many have sought counsel, yet permitted despair to rule their lives. This, even though a loving Brother sounds a universal call,

> *Come unto me, all ye that labour and are heavy laden, and I will give you rest.*
>
> *Take my yoke upon you, and learn of me; for I am meek and lowly in heart: and ye shall find rest unto your souls.*
>
> *For my yoke is easy, and my burden is light.*[11]
>
> *Every soul stands in need of the Savior's mediation, since all are sinners. . . . So great are the difficulties and dangers, so strong is the influence of evil in the world, and so weak is man in resistance thereto, that without the aid of a power above that of humanity no soul would find its way back to God from whom it came. The need of a Redeemer lies in the inability of man to raise himself from the temporal to the spiritual plane, from the lower kingdom to the higher.*
>
> *. . . So, for the advancement of man from his present fallen and relatively degenerate state to the higher condition of spiritual life, a power above his own must cooperate. . . . man may be reached and lifted.*[12]

The Lord's promises and invitation extend to all. But, you must seek Him before you will find Him. One of the greatest stumbling blocks to picking oneself up and obtaining a hope of salvation comes from not recognizing the lies which Satan uses to keep you down. He will say:

1.   You are no good—In fact, you are the world's worst.

---

[11] Matthew 11:28-30.
[12] Talmage, James E. *Jesus the Christ*, Deseret Book, 1949, pp. 26-28.

2.    You cannot talk to Father—Besides He doesn't listen to everybody anyway.

3.    Even if He did listen—You have gone too far to be delivered.

Don't ever believe him. You are a child of God, brought through a noble lineage and endowed with eternal promises.

You alone can make the choice to change where change is needed. If there is need for repentance, put your life in order that your heart may be turned from indulging continually in forbidden pleasures. Then when there is nothing that stands between you and the Lord, this review may help you to stay in the narrow way and obtain the greater blessings promised to those who would have ears to hear and eyes to see. As you read, pray and meditate you will find your place in the plan and can then proceed until the perfect day when the Lord will finally take away the veil and let you look with wonder into eternity.

May you find peace and an abiding testimony of the Lord Jesus Christ. For, there is no gift, blessing or power which you cannot inherit; it is your legal right to claim a part in all the Father has. It will be bestowed through your righteousness and zeal for His cause.

As you read on, the sequence of chapters is designed to lead your mind to understand perhaps a little more clearly who you are, what is expected of you, and gain some insights into some of the things you may accomplish with the time allotted you here in mortality. But before proceeding, would you make your life and its value a matter of sincere prayer and then contemplate the following thoughts.

## Thoughts For Meditation

1.    The Lord has revealed a way to return to His presence.

2.    Perfection is attainable even though weaknesses and impediments must be overcome along the way.

3.    Natural man has to put forth an effort in order to yield to the enticings of the Holy Spirit.

4. I can be like Him, think His thoughts, and obtain His power.

5. "Beginning the way" may be extremely difficult, but it will be worth the effort.

6. All things are possible for the person who learns to believe.

## CHAPTER TWO

# Faith in the Lord

There is an inherent greatness in the soul of each person, and the Gospel plan helps discover and develop this greatness. Oftentimes though, a person does not catch the significant meaning of the Gospel plan and what it can do for him. Some feel that keeping the commandments may be a restriction on their living, when in reality keeping the commandments of the Lord brings forth dignity to an individual, gives greater opportunities for self-fulfillment, and assists one in becoming master of his own soul. One of the most demanding responsibilities in this life is to know more about ourselves, overcome our weaknesses and capitalize on our strengths so that the divine power in each of us can serve as a guiding influence for ourselves and for others.

Heavenly Father does not want His children to become discouraged because of a loss, a defeat or a lack of achievement. His continual desire is to have His children experience true joy in this life. Each must catch a glimpse of the great human and spiritual powers that he possesses, the miraculous capability that is his. However, a veil is drawn before our eyes as we entered mortality, and we do not recognize the godliness that exists within us. Consequently, each person must believe that life has an everlasting purpose and develop a perfect faith in the Lord Jesus Christ.

This faith is a gift given to each man who is exercised in righteous doing, to know of the past, to be able to understand the present, and to know of the future with assurance. Faith leads to final solutions of life's problems and becomes a comforting guide throughout life. Faith is more powerful in human endeavor than judgment or experience itself. Faith is power. When a person does not have faith he generally is filled with doubt. This lack of faith, unfortunately, leads a person to succumb to his weaknesses. When an individual develops faith it must come from the heart; it must be a personal yearning to be in harmony with the Godhead. As a person develops faith he must understand that it is an intricate part of his being, not something that is present only when he walks into the chapel. Something that is part of his everyday living. Each person has the responsibility for the development of this faith; consequently, the responsibility for his own salvation and exaltation.

## The Nature of Faith

All learning is self-learning and must be self-appropriated or self-discovered through the Spirit of the Holy Ghost. Truth cannot be found for an individual, but only by the individual. There is a difference between learning and having an experience. For example, it is one thing to know the map of the road, to know the beauty of the forest, to know how many lakes exist, etc. It is quite another to actually experience drinking from a cool mountain stream, to smelling the aroma from the pine trees. So it is with the Gospel. We can study, we can gain certain information, but the important thing is to experience the Gospel in our lives.

Faith begins by learning to believe. As Jesus said: "If thou canst believe, all things are possible to him that believeth."[1] We can succeed if we learn how to believe. Those who are worried, discouraged, anxious or afraid need to understand this principle. A person may learn to believe through a process similar to learning how to walk. In Mark, we find a father taking his sick son to the Master to be healed, exhibiting the essence of believing. And through faith the son was healed.[2] This principle of faith

---

[1] Mark 9:23.
[2] See Mark 9:17, 29.

which is the first principle of the Gospel, comes about by living righteously, and represents the dynamic power of godliness in man. An abiding faith comes from being active in the Church and doing the Lord's will. It is a continuum that is endless and increases as we participate in the beautiful plan of salvation.

## The Reflection of Faith

The Gospel of Jesus Christ brings forth the greatest joy and happiness possible in this life. The happiness radiates in the very countenances of those who embrace it. We reflect these feelings and attitudes to other people. There was a young man who was attending a certain Christian school and he belonged to that faith. He desired to study violin with a university professor of the L.D.S. faith. The university professor was made to promise he would not indoctrinate this young, promising violinist with Mormonism. This was agreed. During the first lesson the student asked the professor what made him so happy. "It is the Gospel, John." "What do you mean by the Gospel?" asked John. "You will find out in due time," the professor said. During each of the following lessons the student persistently asked the same question about the happiness he seemed to see in the life of the professor. Because of the professor's promise, no discussion was ever held as to what the Gospel was.

Because of deep concern about the revealing aspects of the Gospel, the young violinist sought answers from his Mormon friends. This elevating experience between student and teacher continued as the student appropriated more Gospel principles from as many sources as possible. After a few months' time the violinist asked the professor a favor. "Of course John, whatever you say." Then the exciting question was asked. "It has been due time and I have found out what the Gospel is! Will you come to my baptism?" The professor not only attended the baptism, but also spoke at his missionary farewell a year later. Faith radiates and is perceived by those about us.

Faith comes from right thinking of long cherished associations with godliness or godlike thoughts. The Lord said, "No man can serve two masters: for either he will hate the one, and love the other; or else he will hold to the one, and despise the other. Ye cannot serve God and mammon."[3] Again, the Lord tells us: "Seek ye first the kingdom of God, and his righteousness; and all these things shall be added unto you."[4] Too often an individual does not literally call upon the Lord to help him develop his faith. In James the Lord tells us: "But let him ask in faith, nothing wavering. For he that wavereth is like a wave of the sea driven with the wind and tossed."[5] This great blessing of faith is ours to receive. But in order to receive it we must be sensitive receptors. The Lord tells us: "I, the Lord, am bound when ye do what I say; but when ye do not what I say, ye have no promise."[6]

Through Jesus Christ an eternal plan has been designed to guide every man who will rise above the sensual and devilish nature. Faith is developed by obedience to and gaining experience with this plan. This suggests that individuals must seek experiences that lead to eternal truth and not in conflict with the truth. We must seek intellectual experiences that lead to eternal truth, and not in opposition to it. We must seek moral standards that are consistent with eternal truth. We must seek cultural experiences and personal conduct that lead to truth. This means we must strive for control of passions, appetites, and physical aspects of life so that we can become worthy recipients of all truth.

## The Development of Faith

Perhaps one of the most often asked questions is: How may we have His Spirit to be with us? An answer to this question would be to seek humility. We must probe into our motives, even though this can be disturbing. Some of the basic human motivations have unpleasant names: vanity, rivalry, desire of power, greed, lust, etc. President George Albert Smith, as part of his personal creed, stated: "I would avoid the publicity of high positions and discourage flattery of thoughtless friends."[7] William

---

[3] Matthew 6:24.

[4] Matthew 6:33.

[5] James 1:6.

[6] D&C 82:10.

[7] Smith, George Albert. *The Teachings of George Albert Smith,* Edited by Robert and Susan McIntosh, Salt Lake City, Utah: Bookcraft, 1996. Quoted from *Improvement Era,* May 1851.

Knox contributed the following insightful poem:

> Oh why should the spirit of mortal be proud?
> Like a swift-flitting meteor, a fast-flying cloud,
> A flash of the lightning, a break of the wave,
> Man passeth from life to his rest in the grave.
>
> The maid on whose cheek, on whose brow, in whose eye,
> Shone beauty and pleasure—her triumphs are by'
> And alike from the minds of living erased
> And the memories of mortals who loved her and praised.
>
> The hand of the king, that the scepter hath borne;
> The brow of the priest, that the miser hath worn;
> The eye of the sage, and the heart of the brave,—
> Are hidden and lost in the depths of the grave.
>
> The peasant whose lot was to sow and to reap;
> The herdsman, who climbed with his goats up the steep;
> The beggar, who wandered in search of his bread,—
> Have faded away like the grass that we tread.
>
> The saint who enjoyed the communion of heaven,
> The sinner who dared to remain unforgiven;
> The wise and the foolish, the guilty and just,
> Have quietly mingled their bones in the dust.
>
> Yea! hope and despondency, pleasure and pain,
> Are mingled together in sunshine and rain;
> And the smile and the tear, the song and the dirge,
> Still follow each other like surge upon surge.
>
> 'Tis the wink of an eye, 'tis the draught of a breath,
> From the blossom of health to the paleness of death,
> From the gilded saloon to the bier and the shroud—
> Oh, why should the spirit of mortal be proud?

All worthwhile qualities associated with humility will abide with us for eternities to come. In the dialogues of Plato, Rafael Demos asks: "Is he genuine, does he ring true?" It is terrible to deceive. It is difficult to build back confidence in those who have been deceived. Humility is a condition for service, doing the right things for the right reasons.

Another way to develop faith is to have a true heart. Jesus extolled the pure in heart, they are they who shall see God.[8] This gives a peace of mind, a clear conscience, and allows the Spirit of the Lord to dwell joyously within us. There is only one person who can harm you—yourself. We can improve and learn from our mistakes if we are humble, regardless of the nature of the task. All living mortals have weaknesses and imperfections, but some are more serious than others. Robert Louis Stevenson has said: "You cannot run away from a weakness, you must sometime fight it out or perish; and if this be so, why not now and where you stand."[9]

### The Nature of Repentance

One of the greatest principles given to mankind by the Savior was that of repentance. No one wants to be burdened down because of weaknesses or imperfections. But because of a lack of understanding of the great principle of repentance, and because of a lack of knowing of the love our Lord has for us, oftentimes we hesitate to exercise the principle of free agency in repenting and eliminating these weaknesses. These weaknesses can only cause an impediment to the spirit, and when we do not have the Spirit of the Lord with us, faith is weakened.

To actually know and experience how much the Lord loves us is almost an impossibility. The nearest comparison we could make would be the deep love parents have for their own children. This type of love is indescribable, but may be experienced where there is true love and joy in the home. However, since we are mortal parents with mortal bodies and not the creators of the spirit, we can only say that we are part creators. And thus, can only feel a portion of this eternal love. One of the constant pursuits in this life should be to understand this principle of love and to know how much our Savior and Heavenly Father really do love us.

We have a tendency, though, to retain weaknesses and imperfections

---

[8] See Matthew 5:8.
[9] *Essays of Travel*, Chapter 1, The Amateur Emigrant, [1916].

as millstones around our necks. If only we could understand that these need not remain with us any longer than it takes to become humble and understand the principle of repentance and take sufficient action for proper elimination. Repentance is only disappointing when incomplete. President Spencer W. Kimball has suggested the following procedures for true repentance:

1. Recognition and desire to repent.

2. Regret and remorse (broken heart and contrite spirit).

3. Unwavering resolution to cease whatever the imperfection may be.

4. Forgiveness from the Lord.

5. Forgiveness from the Lord's Church through His servant.

We must realize that restitution is required in repentance and that we must do the will of the Lord. Many people do not realize the importance of visiting with the bishop in regards to serious problems of transgression. We recognize that only God can completely forgive one who trespasses against His mortal law; however, the bishop is the ecclesiastical authority and represents the Church as an ordained judge in Israel. For this reason, we must go to the bishop because he is the Lord's representative. He holds the keys. People carry their serious transgressions burdensomely year after year and never feel free of them until they have confessed them to their bishop. The Lord has said: "Behold, he who has repented of his sins, the same is forgiven, and I, the Lord, remember them no more. By this ye may know if a man repenteth of his sins—behold, he will confess them and forsaketh them."[10] In Proverbs we read: "He that covereth his sins shall not prosper: but whoso confesseth and forsaketh them shall have mercy."[11]

In this principle of remission, there are two forgivenesses that must occur, one from the Lord and the other from the Lord's Church through His

---

[10] D&C 58:42-43. See also Isaiah 55:6-7, 1:18.
[11] Proverbs 28:13.

leaders. As one feels a broken heart and a contrite spirit, as did Enos,[12] he should go to the Lord in mighty prayer and continue this petition until he receives an assurance that his sins have been forgiven. A bishop claims no authority to absolve sins, but he does assure pardon, waive penalties, relieve tension and may assure continuation of activity.

Once a person has repented and obtained forgiveness, it should not be necessary for him to discuss his transgressions before other authorities. He need not carry guilt complexes and feel that he must repeat his past confessions of sin when confronted by future bishops and stake presidents. There might be exceptions to this where priesthood authorities are impressed to inquire about your worthiness. Perhaps one might answer when interviewed again by saying, "Yes, I am morally clean. I have made mistakes, but have made this right with the proper Church authority, and have lived a clean life since."

## The Role of the Bishop

Often, members of the Church ask, "Why go to the bishop?" In the first place, this is a consistent, orderly plan and we go because we have been asked to do so. Second, we are able to pull out from the very core of the complete problem that is festering inside. This causes a great release of strain. Third, the bishop will be able to help correct the problem, whether it be a problem of morality, word of wisdom, tithing, etc. Fourth, there is a spirit that causes a person to feel cleansed. Fifth, in further interviews one will have a clear conscience.

The old story of "the nail in the board" is false doctrine. This illustration has been used to suggest that once the nail is pulled out there is always a hole left in the board. If we really have faith in repentance, we know that once a person has repented and is forgiven it is literally as though he had not done it. This imperfection is erased from the records of heaven and remembered no more. Satan will want to continue to make us feel unworthy, however. He will say: "You are no good." "You are unclean." "You are unworthy." We must exercise great discipline on our

---

[12] Enos 4-5.

part to crush this type of thinking and realize how much the Lord wants us to succeed. The time will come when these bad memories will be erased completely.

This is a part of the principle of forgiveness. We make our own prisons, and we are our own jailkeepers. We have the choice of slavery or of freedom. Sometimes slavery is chosen because the principle of repentance is not understood or properly acted upon. An unknown author reminds us: "Today is the day I have been looking for. All my life has been spent in preparation for it. Yesterday and tomorrow are far away nothings. The one a faint memory, the other a vague promise. This is my day. It offers all that God has to give, and I am a laggard and a coward if I fail to make the most of it."

## The Fruits of Faith

One of the best ways to have an abiding faith is to live the Gospel in its fullness. Many expect all of the blessings from the Gospel with only partial participation. Yet, many are satisfied with partial home teaching, with irregular family home evenings, a partial tithe, non-observance of fast day, infrequent prayer, or deny oneself the joy of temple marriage. Joy comes from partaking of the Gospel in its fullness. Our Heavenly Father wants us to know joy and experience this frequently with as much depth as mortality allows. The Gospel of Jesus Christ we embrace is sacred, holy, and eternal. No part of the glorified plan can be cast off by saying, "I have no need of thee." The fullness of the Gospel is here for all of us. There is no Gospel facet that is not ultimately helpful. When we do not participate in the complete plan, we are the losers; our spirits have been denied that growth, and our faith becomes weaker.

Those who strike back or who have taken offense and say they will not go to Sacrament meeting or keep the commandments because of supposed offenses are only hurting themselves. In the long run, the easiest thing would be to completely partake of the Gospel. Satan beguiles us by saying it is easier to succumb to social pressures than to abide by the Master's plan. What a choice blessing to live when the fullness of the Gospel is on the earth! We must prepare a people worthy to live with Christ when He comes. When we violate any part of the plan the Savior has given us, we will suffer the consequences. These causes and consequences are referred to in the scriptures as the "Law of the Harvest." Dwarfing our own powers for progress and blighting our own prospects for achievement are aspects we must avoid. Faith is a gift that is individually earned. It is not an inheritance.

## Faith and Commitment

As faith continues to grow, we develop a commitment in regards to the Gospel such as the young man who entered college from the mission field in Kentucky where he had developed a strong testimony of the Gospel. For many years he had been afflicted by a speech impediment and had been waiting for the opportunity to have a bishop of the church give him a special blessing. His father was not a member of the church. The first Sunday on campus he made an appointment with his bishop and said, "I would like to have a special blessing to remove my speech impediment." The bishop, recognizing the great testimony and power of faith that this individual possessed, arranged for a special blessing to be given which would be preceded by fasting. When this young man was given this special blessing the Lord's Spirit was so strong that both could feel the strength from their bodies being lifted and the young man was promised through the power of the priesthood that his speech impediment would be removed. With the great faith that he possessed, through the blessing of the Lord, this young man left with his speech impediment corrected. All things are possible to them who believe.

There was a young Latter-day Saint girl who became the representative from her state to a Miss American pageant, who also had great faith. As the result of an accident the end of her spine had been broken. She recognized the power and influence of the priesthood and called upon her bishop for a special blessing. She felt she could not at that particular time be in bed so long. In her blessing she was promised she would be healed immediately through her faith and by the power of the priesthood. The doctors examined and x-rayed this young girl the next morning and found that her spine was healed.

Such meaningful experiences, coupled with a realization of the source of all good gifts, lead to powerful personal testimonies and provide the courage to remain steadfast in the faith. While belief is a product of our mind, faith comes from the heart. Faith that comes from the heart has a compelling nature that literally pulls a person closer to his own eternal glory. As the Lord declared, "Thy faith hath made thee whole."[13]

## Thoughts For Meditation

1. Faith in the Lord Jesus Christ leads to the greatest joy and happiness possible in this life.

2. A motivating faith can be mine when I become a sensitive receptor to the Spirit of the Holy Ghost.

3. There is a perceptible difference in the countenance of the soul who develops faith through overcoming his weaknesses.

4. Faith is a gift that is individually earned and not an inheritance.

5. Through exercising faith I will be blessed with an abiding testimony in the Lord Jesus Christ.

---

[13] Mark 5:34, Luke 8:48, Enos 1:8.

CHAPTER THREE

# The Pillars of Testimony*

Atestimony is that precious gift that enables a person to have enduring faith in Christ. It is what the North Star is to the mariner, what the keel is to a sailing boat, what the track is to a train. A testimony makes progress in the right direction possible. It is not progress itself, but it is indispensable to any spiritual progress. Faith and testimony grow together.

A testimony of Jesus Christ, of His gospel and of His work, is composed of three essential ingredients. The first of these is a recognition of spiritual experience; the second is an understanding of the Lord's words and work; and the third is having experienced the fruits, the rewards of faith.

## Recognizing the Spiritual

Spiritual experience is fundamental to everything connected with the gospel of Jesus Christ. It is not something mysterious or mystical as some would tell us, nor is it rare and difficult to obtain as others would say. Spiritual experiences are quite ordinary and quite abundant in the world.

*Dr. Chauncey C. Riddle, former Dean of the Brigham Young University Graduate School, is the author of this chapter "The Pillars of Testimony." Gratitude is expressed to dean Riddle for his willingness to share his ideas in this book with the authors and readers.

They are so commonplace it is like the air we breathe, for spiritual experience is the experience of a spirit, our own spirit. It is the inner consciousness that each of us enjoys. We all have thoughts, ideas, hopes, and fears that are not related to what is coming in from the outside of our bodies. The realm of spiritual experience is the privacy of the mind.

That we each have spiritual experience is ordinary. What is extraordinary is when any one of us becomes a keen judge, a connoisseur of the things that are found within the privacy of our minds. What a testimony requires is the recognition that in our minds there do occur impulses to do what we feel is good and prohibitions against that which we, ourselves, know to be bad. Another name for this requirement is honesty of conscience, the ability to admit that we are influenced in a way which we know to be good but which is contrary to our desires. It is this precious honesty or recognition of spiritual enticements to do good that is essential to a testimony.

## Knowing the Savior

The understanding one must enjoy to have a real testimony has its central focus on the Savior. To know who He is, where He came from, and what His authority is, and to know of His earthly mission are crucial. Then we can understand His gospel and the message of hope that it brings. Then we can understand His Church and see its operations in each dispensation as the unfolding of a divine plan culminating in what is happening in our own wards and stakes today. We will then see why moral standards are so critical to righteousness and why one cannot love his neighbor purely until he loves God with that pure obedience called faith. This knowledge will likely come from the scriptures, but in written or oral form it must come from those who are authorized servants of God, men who know what they are talking about. This requirement for a testimony is reflected in the statement of our hymn, "How firm a foundation, ye Saints of the Lord, is laid for your faith in his excellent word!"[1]

---

[1] How Firm A Foundation, *Hymns*, 1985, #85.

## Fruits of Faith

The third component necessary to a testimony is to have in our lives and memories the fruits of faith in Christ. This is called, in the parlance of the world, a pragmatic evidence. And the gospel is pragmatic. The Lord said try me; see if faith in me does bring that precious inner peace for which you long. And many there be who have tried the Lord and have found Him not to be wanting.

These then are the components of testimony. First, an ability to hear the voice of the Lord when He guides us to righteousness; this we called recognition of spiritual experience. Second, knowledge of the work and ways of God; this we might call understanding. Third, having in our lives that most precious fruit of the gospel, the quiet inner peace that passeth understanding.

## The Parable of The Sower

The Savior gives us a graphic illustration of these three elements in the parable of the sower. He tells us what would happen if we were to lack any one of these elements.

> *A sower went out to sow his seed: and as he sowed, some fell by the way side; and it was trodden down, and the fowls of the air devoured it.*[2]

The Savior explained this as follows:

The seed is the word of God.

> *Those by the way side are they that hear; then cometh the devil, and taketh away the word out of their hearts, lest they should believe and be saved.*[3]

These people off the beaten path are those of the world who are so trodden down by the influences of the world that they do not recognize the

---

[2] Luke 8:5.
[3] Luke 8:11-12.

word of the Lord when it comes to them. When the word of the Lord comes to any man, it is carried by the Holy Spirit into his heart. But perhaps that man pays little attention to his heart, priding himself on being objective in responding only to "hard, cold physical evidence" which affects his body and which he can demonstrate publicly to others. If so, the precious things in his heart lie undiscriminated, unsorted. As time passes, it is easy for the adversary to snatch the precious word of the Lord from his memory. So, for want of attention and honest recognition of admitted worth, the word of the Lord is lost from consciousness and the opportunity to have a testimony and be saved is gone.

Returning to the Savior's parable, we see the second error.

> *And some (seed) fell upon a rock; and as soon as it was sprung up, it withered away, because it lacked moisture.*[4]

This is interpreted by the Savior as follows:

> *They on the rock are they, which, when they hear, receive the word with joy; and these have no root, which for a while believe, and in time of temptation fall away.*[5]

These are persons who are able to recognize and treasure the word of the Lord. They begin to keep His commandments; yet they do not understand His work. In the face of temptation they wither because they cannot see the purpose and necessity of being different from the world, of keeping themselves pure and unspotted. Lacking the perspective of eternity, they fall easy prey to the desires of the moment, and the joy of the word of the Lord is overwhelmed by the lusts of the flesh. Had they searched in the scriptures and listened carefully to their priesthood leaders, they would have caught the point of sacrifice and they would have had the hope of the rewards of righteousness. This would have nourished their souls in the hot glare of temptation. But lacking root, not understanding what they were doing, they withered.

---

[4] Luke 8:6.
[5] Luke 8:13.

The third problem is represented in the teaching of our Savior as follows:

> *And some (seed) fell among thorns; and the thorns*
> *sprang up with it, and choked it. . . .*
>
> *And that which fell among thorns are they, which,*
> *when they have heard, go forth, and are choked with*
> *cares and riches and pleasures of this life, and bring*
> *no fruit to perfection.*[6]

This is the problem of what it is that satisfies us. Some persons hear the gospel message but are quite content with the world the way it is. They busy themselves with making and preserving their wealth and in living deliciously; they see no reason for a change. This is the problem of the upper economic classes of society especially. The Book of Mormon speaks of them being comforted with carnal security and thus being carefully led away down to hell.[7] If they are ill, they have the best doctors; if they are hungry, they command the finest cuisine; if they are lonely, they throw a party; if they are depressed or nervous, they are soothed by drugs, tobacco, alcohol, or whatever suits their fancy. They fancy, of course, that they do not need a Savior. Whatever they need, they can get—they think. These persons seldom gain testimonies until their health and wealth are taken from them. Bereaved of the temporal salvation they have so ignorantly enjoyed, they begin to glimpse the fact that there might be something better to life than just satisfying the flesh.

## The Gospel Produces Good Fruit

Undoubtedly there are some persons who do not have the fruits of the gospel in their lives simply because of not knowing what they are missing. My neighbor has a nectarine tree. He enjoyed its abundant fruit each year until he tasted one of the nectarines on my tree. Now his taste terrible, and he has grafted in many twigs from my tree hoping to convert his into a tree that produces good fruit.

---

[6] Luke 8:7, 14.
[7] 2 Nephi 28:21.

Producing good fruit is the point of the gospel. If we live the gospel, our lives produce love, kindness, charity; we produce righteousness. Righteousness is caring more to see others happy than worrying about our own happiness. This is one of the paradoxes of the gospel. The only way to be really happy is to forget about our own happiness and to labor diligently for the happiness of others. The Savior said:

> *He that findeth his life shall lose it: and he that*
> *loseth his life for my sake shall find it.*[8]

Above all, our God is a God of righteousness. Whatever we do for His sake, we do in the cause of righteousness. And, among those who have tasted the fruits of righteousness which have come through obedience to Christ, there are those who desire this fruit above all else. It is even more important than life itself to them. These are they who have strong, secure testimonies of the gospel, of the Savior. They know the gospel is true because when they heard the word of the Lord they had a spiritual quickening. Through this spiritual experience, they gained insight into the work of the Lord, the work of righteousness. And, when through faith they acted in obedience to that understanding, they tasted the precious fruit of the tree of life and knew of God's goodness and love. Then they were founded on the rock. Then they had an anchor for their souls. These are they of whom the Savior said:

> *And other (seed) fell upon good ground, and*
> *sprang up, and bare fruit in hundredfold. . . .*
>
> *But that on the good ground are they, which in an*
> *honest and good heart, having heard the word, keep it,*
> *and bring forth fruit with patience.*[9]

## Testimonies and Righteousness

One plain and very important conclusion we may draw from the Savior's parable is that testimonies are not for everyone. There will come a day when every knee shall bow and every tongue confess, but today only

---

[8] Matthew 10:39.
[9] Luke 8:8, 15.

those who have honest and good hearts can be sure of gaining a testimony, and they gain one because they love righteousness. That love of righteousness leads them to the Savior, because only in and through Him are they able to bring forth true fruits of righteousness. He is the way, the truth, and the life.

We have seen in the example of the Savior's parable of the sower what happens when we leave out one of the necessary elements in gaining a testimony. Let us observe the consequence of trying to depend upon only one of these elements.

## Spiritual Imitations

Rather frequently there are manifest in our society persons who claim to be spiritual. They have had some unusual experience which has caused them to embark on a crusade or to alter their way of life. With all seeming sincerity they claim to have discovered the truth, which supposed truth they pursue with great zeal. When we see this claim to spiritual manifestation and its attendant zeal, we ought to check carefully for the other two aspects of true testimony. First, does this spirituality this person claims to have bring him understanding? Does it ring true in comparison with what the scriptures tell us? Is it consistent with the advice and counsel of the authorities of the Church? Secondly, does it bring forth in that person's life the works and fruits of righteousness: love, kindness, joy, peace?

The Savior has given us a measure by which to judge those who claim to be spiritual. "By their fruits ye shall know them."[10] It takes very little experience to separate good fruits from bad fruits if we are doing careful thinking. The reason for bad fruits and for being very wary of those who claim special spiritual experience is that Satan produces his own revelation of experience abundantly in the world. Many, many of those who think they have found the Lord have simply lent an ear to Satan. Undoubtedly, only those who are honest and good in heart can detect all spurious revelation, that is to say, revelation not from God.

---

[10] Matthew 7:20.

Detecting Spurious Revelation

But there are rational means for detecting spurious revelation. Recognizing that a rational formula is no substitute for long experience in any field, we might note the following marks which are associated with people who have had false revelation.

1.    Indiscriminate recounting of the spiritual experience. (The Savior told us not to cast our pearls.)

2.    Insisting that others accept this spiritual experience. (In the Lord's system each person depends on his own personal revelation.)

3.    Inconsistency of the supposed revelation with scripture and with the words of the living prophets. (The Lord has told us that His house is a house of order.)

4.    Fruits of unhappiness, contention, hate, confusion. (For the Lord's way is light, truth, simplicity, and unity.)

There is no shortage of revelation in this world. The problem is to tell that which is true revelation given of the Lord, from that which is spurious revelation, given of the adversary.

Knowing or Living

Let's turn now to an examination of what happens when a person attempts to base his testimony solely on a knowledge or understanding of the gospel. We occasionally see a person who has read all the books and has accumulated a tremendous store of catechistic answers to questions about religious matters. When challenged on a point, the person uses the method of proof-texting; that is, he produces scriptures and quotations which purportedly substantiate his opinion. This person is in the tradition of the scribes and pharisees whom the Savior so roundly scored because they delighted in knowing the words about the work of God rather than in living by the word of God.

Many times this person who has only great knowledge has correct answers. He will quote scripture and propound the words of the prophets at great length. His problem is that it all comes from his head and not from his heart. It is sometimes said that this person has an intellectual testimony, which is to say, he is fascinated by the rational unity and consistency of the gospel and the scriptures. But this fascination is not a true testimony. It is only an intellectual game which the person is playing. Anyone who is said to be "intellectually" converted to the Church is not founded on the rock. Soon some other intellectual game will fascinate him more, and he will be as zealous and catechistic about it as he was about the gospel. Or perhaps the Brethren will ordain certain of the seventy to be high priests, or they might put five counselors in the First Presidency, or perhaps they might even do away with one or more of the auxiliaries of the Church. These persons are then offended because the work of a former president of the Church is being countermanded. They see this as an inconsistency, and their intellectual house of cards is toppled. They forget that the original instruction was given spiritually, by revelation; that the change is given spiritually, by revelation; and that a member of the Church can appropriately sustain either or both only by means of his own personal revelation.

But the person who glories only in knowing about the kingdom of God does not enjoy personal revelation from the Lord. And because he does not live the gospel, which he cannot do without personal revelation, he does not have the special fruits of the Spirit in his life. He will not and cannot endure in the kingdom unless he repents and adds those missing dimensions to his life.

## And Signs There Are

Turning now to the third possibility, we see the case of the person who settles for the fruits only, who has no spirituality nor depth of understanding in his life. This is the person who depends upon signs. And signs there are. Signs follow those who believe in Christ. Signs also follow those who knowingly or unknowingly serve Satan. The signs of these two masters are not always the same, but they are not always different. Thus a person who depends on signs alone has no true idea as to what or who might be the cause of the signs on which he depends.

It is not unusual to see in the Church a person who believes the Church is true because he was there when Aunt Annie was administered to by the priesthood and was miraculously healed. He saw them lay on hands; he saw Aunt Annie healed. Is that not proof enough? It is for him. Building his house on the sand, he proceeds as if he had a testimony. But then Aunt Annie becomes ill again. She is administered again, but this time passes on. Everyone is grief stricken at losing beloved Aunt Annie. But our friend who based his testimony on her healing is not only grief stricken, he is terrified. He thinks that maybe the gospel is not true; perhaps there is no God; perhaps life is just a monstrous joke of nature. Because he has not accepted into his life the comforts and guidance of the Spirit of the Lord, he does not and cannot know why Aunt Annie was restored on the one occasion and released on the other. He does not have the understanding of the gospel to know that death is not a curse but a blessing to the righteous. Bereaved of moorings, our friend is swept with the tide of skepticism and despair, now despising the sandy foundation which once supported his unstable house of testimony.

## Testimony and Faith

It has been obvious that testimony and faith are very closely associated in the gospel of Jesus Christ. What we have here called testimony is very close to what Paul talks about when he discusses faith in the Book of Hebrews: The formula we have given sounds very much like Alma's description of how to gain faith. The connection is that testimony is the necessary prerequisite to sustained faith. Testimony is the basis, the foundation for acting on faith. A testimony is knowing that the gospel is true. Knowing that, one can then exercise great faith.

To exercise faith in Jesus Christ, one must hear the words of Christ. These come to us in the still, small voice of His Spirit. If we then believe and obey the Savior, we are showing forth faith in Him. But a person cannot go very far acting on faith, not far enough to save his soul, without knowing that the course he is pursuing is the will of God. Without that knowledge it is too risky and expensive to act on faith. The sacrifices demanded are too great. A sandy foundation will not support them. But when we have tried our God and know that He is just and true and righteous, then we can exercise faith in Him, unto death if necessary, because we have a testimony.

On the other hand, one may have a testimony and not continue to act in faith. This is the terrible route that apostates of every dispensation have taken. Having known the goodness of the Lord, they chose to stand apart, to forsake the ways of righteousness, and to return to the world and to sin. A testimony never impels a person to be righteous; it only enables him so to act. The devils all have testimonies of Christ. They know Him and know who He is, but they deliberately choose the way of sin because their hearts are not honest and good.

The scriptures plainly reveal to us that testimony and faith must grow together before either is strong or of great value. The beginning point is always personal revelation for the Lord always takes the first step by extending the arms of mercy towards a man. The man must desire to believe and hope to find righteousness enough to try the Lord, to try the experiment of obeying Him and His words. If a man obeys the Lord, he receives a reward, a spiritual reward. This reward shows him that it is good to obey God. Thus, as a man adds obedience to spirituality, understanding to obedience, and recognizes the result, he has a testimony. As he is further obedient, he gains more understanding and more rewards which increase his testimony. As his testimony grows, he can stand greater and greater spiritual manifestations. As he obeys the instructions from the Lord given in these revelations, his faith becomes greater and greater. Thus these two, faith and testimony grow together as the saving grace of our Savior until that person has overcome the world.

Perhaps you have watched concrete being poured. In any job that is intended to be strong and lasting, reinforcing steel is placed at strategic intervals. This steel makes the concrete almost indestructible. It may crack and the surface may chip, but the mass remains solid and steadfast. If you have watched somebody trying to destroy reinforced concrete, you know that the simplest thing to do usually is just to pick up the whole mass and cart it off.

Concrete is like faith. A testimony is like reinforcing steel. Satan is the destroyer trying to smash your faith. If you are full of reinforcing steel,

Satan cannot smash you. He would like to take you up bodily and cast you away. But our Savior does not give him that power. So Satan hunts for faith without testimony, for good acts, obedient acts where the person is not sure whom he is obeying, why he is obeying, and if it is worthwhile to obey. When he finds such a person, he puts the pressure on. Not necessarily great massive pressure—just enough to chip off a corner. And then another corner. Here a piece, there a piece, the person is destroyed all the while trying to do what is right. Trying but not succeeding—because of only half trying. Trying to live the gospel without searching the things of the Spirit, without pondering the meaning of the Lord's message, without keenly observing the fruits of the Spirit. To try to have faith without a testimony is to be thoughtless. But to think, to search, to obey, to experiment, to find that rock upon which to build, that is thinking, the best kind of thinking; it is called repentance. And that kind of thinking is real living; in fact, it is the beginning of eternal life.

## Testimony Bearing

A word about the bearing of testimony. In one sense a testimony is a wholly private thing. It is something you know, it is part of your life, your conscience, your experience, but you cannot show it to anyone else because it is part of your inner life and experience, your spiritual life. That, of course, is why it is so valuable to you. It is your personal comfort and warrant for your faith. No matter what happens to anyone else, you have something you know for sure about spiritual matters. You and the Lord have a functioning, ongoing relationship and companionship.

The privacy of your testimony is another witness to your personal free agency. Because it is private, other persons cannot judge you nor assist you in your thinking. You must think through the evidence for yourself. It is your own personal evidence. Others may check your reasoning, but they cannot check either your data or your desires. So you remain free of men because of your privacy, and free from the flesh because these data are spiritual. This is the freedom which the gospel offers to all who seek the truth.

But though your testimony is private, the Lord does not always want you to keep hidden the fact that you have one. Under His guidance you are to bear your testimony. When He prompts you, He wants you to express to others the fact that you have one, as Paul says, to give account to men of the hope that is within you. You can never give another person your testimony, or even a testimony. But there are times when you must stand up to be counted.

For when you bear your testimony, you declare yourself to be on the side of the Savior. You express to men that you have tried the Lord and found Him to be good, and you stand as a personal witness to that truth. As you speak, truly the Holy Ghost is your companion. He, the Holy Ghost also bears His witness to the souls of your hearers. He is a God; His witness is divine. His witness is the beginning of spiritual life, the basis of testimony, the opportunity for faith. While your witness is nothing so grand and mighty as that of the Holy Ghost, nevertheless your witness is the occasion and opportunity for His witness. Thus you are an important and even indispensable part of the Savior's plan to save mankind. If no man bore true witness of God, the occasions for revelation from God would be so sharply diminished as to throw the world into another black night of apostasy. So we are sent into the world to be witnesses of the light. We are not the light. But we know Him and bear testimony of Him; He is Jesus Christ.

Riddle, Chauncey C., The Pillars of Testimony, *Speeches of the Year*, Brigham Young University, June 30, 1970, pp. 2-10. Used through the courtesy of the Brigham Young University Press and the author.

## Thoughts for Meditation

1.   Testimony is the "guiding star" which leads to a knowledge of God and full conversion.

2.   Spiritual experiences may be so plentiful and natural that we may not recognize them as coming from the Lord.

3.   The "precious inner peace" for which you so much long comes from a testimony and faith in the Lord.

4.   A testimony will enable me to act on faith and bring forth good fruit.

5.   Faith and testimony will help me to learn more about the
     Lord's gospel plan and guide me in obtaining revelation
     through "feasting upon His Word."

# CHAPTER FOUR

# Feasting Upon the Words of Christ

After committing oneself to the Lord and receiving the prescribed ordinances at the hand of one having authority, there can come a rich outpouring of guidance and instruction. Testimony is strengthened and magnified. Oftentimes though, we are prone to stop short of these promised blessings and be satisfied with far less light than that which is available. Nephi pointed to this tendency when he wrote:

> And now, my beloved brethren, after ye have gotten into this strait and narrow path, I would ask if all is done? Behold, I say unto you, Nay; for ye have not come thus far save it were by the word of Christ with unshaken faith in him, relaying wholly upon the merits of him who is mighty to save.
>
> Wherefore, ye must press forward with a steadfastness in Christ, having a perfect brightness of hope, a love of God and of all men. Wherefore, if ye shall press forward, feasting upon the word of Christ, and endure to the end, behold, thus saith the Father:

39

*Ye shall have eternal life.*[1]

Then Nephi went on to explain how the will of the Lord is revealed:

> *Do ye not remember that I said unto you that after ye had received the Holy Ghost ye could speak with the tongue of angels? . . .*
>
> *Angels speak by the power of the Holy Ghost; wherefore, they speak the words of Christ. Wherefore, I said unto you, feast upon the words of Christ; for behold, the words of Christ will tell you things what ye should do.*
>
> *For behold, again I say unto you that if ye will enter in by the way, and receive the Holy Ghost, it will show unto you all things what ye should do.*[2]

What a thrilling promise!

## Being Guided by the Spirit

I had been given a sabbatical leave for a year to secure my doctorate. After a great deal of prayer and knowing we had very little money, we called upon the Lord to bless us. We prayed fervently for the Spirit of the Lord to direct us because I knew how expensive housing would be, and we knew that we needed the right school arrangement for our children. After traveling to the metropolitan area of Los Angeles during the day, the Spirit prompted me to stop in the little town of Maywood, California, and to call upon the Bishop. His address was in the telephone book, and I went to his home. A charming lady came to the door. I told her that I wanted to see the Bishop and she said, "Won't you come in. I will call him." The Bishop was a doctor and indicated to his wife that I should not leave. He would be there immediately.

On his arrival he said, "You're an answer to my prayer."

I said, "I thought you were an answer to my prayer."

---

[1] 2 Nephi 31:19-20.
[2] 2 Nephi 32:2-3, 5.

He said, "No, for three months now I have needed a Secretary for the Senior Aaronic Priesthood Program in our ward. We have one active and thirty-two inactive adult Aaronic Priesthood holders."

He said, "For the past two months I have told the Stake President I would find a man. On my last report I indicated at the bottom of the report that I would have a man by the first of September.

"Now, this is the first of September. What has been your experience in the Church?" These good people took us in with open arms. We served the Lord in every way we could. They arranged a small home for a modest cost and literally helped us move in so that we could financially make it through the year. What a blessing we had in that particular ward. There were sixteen of those men who were sealed to their wives and their lovely children in the Temple within one years' time. They assumed major roles of leadership in the ward and stake.

During that year what a blessing it was to have to be frugal, yet know the Lord would bless us. There were many times with no food in the icebox, but in the morning at 6:00 a.m. there would be a crate of vegetables and fruits for us on our doorstep.

We can be prompted as to things we might do to successfully meet the challenges of mortal life. We will be cared for and watched over. We need not walk or perish in darkness, except by our own choosing. There is a source of inspiration promised to each; which, if we will use it, can guide us in the many decisions which must be made each day. The scriptures do not suggest that this guidance is limited only to matters that are spiritual in nature, although it is most appropriate that first emphasis be placed on matters that pertain to the redemption of man. If you will seek the kingdom of God, and to further the cause of Zion, all things will be added unto you.[3] The Lord, in the Sermon on the Mount, gave this promise: "Blessed are they which do hunger and thirst after righteousness: for they shall be filled."[4]

---

[3] Matthew 6:33.
[4] Matthew 5:6.

Since the Holy Ghost may be referred to as having a "corner on knowledge," it would seem wise to so order our lives that He might abide with us and be a constant companion. At one time President David O. McKay encouraged students not to study on the Sabbath and promised that certain blessings would follow. For many years I had practiced this principle and found it to be true. As bishop of a campus ward, I felt impressed during a Sacrament Meeting to promise the members of the ward that if they would not study on Sunday, and would keep that day holy, the Lord would bless them in their academic pursuits and that they would experience more frequent guidance from the Holy Ghost in all things. I felt further to promise that if they would do this their grades would improve. There were many subsequently who bore their testimonies that it worked.

During my own final doctoral oral examination, I found that many answers came to my mind which I had not previously analyzed in the context of the question asked. This does not mean there was a lack of preparation, but it does suggest that if we will keep close to the Lord, do all that we can, we will be supported in every hour of need. Surely there is nothing which will be withheld from us, which is for our good, if we are living consistent with principles upon which they may be obtained. Why try to learn all of this alone?

## The Well of Living Water

Although an important source of information, we are often too content to spend our lives learning from others. When this is done one seldom experiences the excitement of personal revelation. Unless a person in this condition returns constantly for additional encouragement, he feels a "let-down" spiritually. A wise man once said, "There is a difference between the learned man who will pump you full of knowledge and the one who can give you the key to the well." The former often seeks to surround himself with disciples to test out his opinions and theories; while the latter possesses the ability to lead the learner to eternal sources. Once the key is found, sources of knowledge are found to be never-ending and can be acquired without a mortal teacher. The Prophet Joseph commented that if we could but look into heaven for a few minutes, we would know more than all that has ever been written about the subject.

It has never been the Lord's desire that knowledge be withheld. It has only been when the children of men would not surrender themselves to the enticements of the Spirit that the heavens were closed. To the obedient He said:

> *. . . Unto him that keepeth my commandments I will give the mysteries of my kingdom, and the same shall be in him a well of living water, springing up unto everlasting life.*[5]

Jesus speaking to the woman of Samaria, pointed out that those partaking of the water she gave would thirst again.

> *But whosoever drinketh of the water that I shall give him shall never thirst; but the water that I shall give him shall be in him a well of water springing up into everlasting life.*[6]

The Lord projected the condition of those who would eventually overcome the world and be permitted to partake freely from the fountainhead.

> *. . . These are they which come out of great tribulation, and have washed their robes, and made them white in the blood of the Lamb.*
>
> *Therefore are they before the throne of God, and serve him day and night in his temple: and he that sitteth on the throne shall dwell among them.*
>
> *They shall hunger no more, neither thirst any more; neither shall the sun light on them, nor any heat.*
>
> *For the Lamb which is in the midst of the throne shall feed them, and shall lead them unto living fountains of waters: and God shall wipe away all tears from their eyes.*[7]

---

[5] D&C 63:23.
[6] John 4:14.
[7] Revelations 7:14-17.

The Lord will not withhold any of His mighty words from those who worthily seek His face. But it would prove to be a condemnation to them if light and knowledge were given before acquiring sufficient strength to bear it and learn the requirements of its possession. Alma explained the conditions for learning very well when responding to Zeezrom.

> *. . . It is given unto many to know the mysteries of God; nevertheless they are laid under a strict command that they shall not impart only according to the portion of his word which he doth grant unto the children of men, according to the heed and diligence which they give unto him.*
>
> *And therefore, he that will harden his heart, the same receiveth the lesser portion of the word; and he that will not harden his heart, to him is given the greater portion of the word, until it is given unto him to know the mysteries of God until he knows them in full.*
>
> *And they that will harden their hearts, to them is given the lesser portion of the word until they know nothing concerning his mysteries; and then they are taken captive by the devil, and led by his will down to destruction. Now this is what is meant by the chains of hell.*[8]

## They Shall be Filled

An interesting phenomenon found several places in the scriptures is that at times when something really exciting happened in the lives of certain brethren, they were given a strict command not to write it. It seems almost as though we are given just enough to really make us desire more and then something like this is recorded.

> *. . . behold, I, Nephi, am forbidden that I should write the remainder of the things which I saw and heard; . . . and I have written but a small part of the*

---

[8] Alma 12:9-11.

*things which I saw.*[9]

On other occasions the manifestation of the Lord's power and the beauty of the things seen could not be recorded.

> . . . *and they were caught up into the heaven, and saw and heard unspeakable things.*
>
> *And it was forbidden them that they should utter; neither was it given unto them power that they could utter the things that they saw and heard.*[10]

A more recent experience suggests that although that which is seen cannot be recorded, it is available upon certain conditions and may come to us as a by-product of our faithfulness. The Prophet Joseph Smith and Sidney Rigdon after seeing the three degrees of glory known as "The Vision," recorded that:

> . . . *great and marvelous are the works of the Lord, and the mysteries of his kingdom which he showed unto us, which surpass all understanding in glory, and in might, and in dominion;*
>
> *Which he commanded us we should not write while we were yet in the Spirit, and are not lawful for man to utter;*
>
> *Neither is man capable to make them known, for they are only to be seen and understood by the power of the Holy Spirit, which God bestows on those who love him, and purify themselves before him;*
>
> *To whom he grants this privilege of seeing and knowing for themselves.*[11]

## Knowing for Oneself

Those who put off the natural man and yield their hearts to the Lord will receive knowledge of eternity line upon line, until in the end they may

---

[9] 1 Nephi 14:28.
[10] 3 Nephi 28:13-14.
[11] D&C 76:114-117.

have a fullness. As promised, the righteous who hunger and thirst shall be filled. But

> *. . . the natural man receiveth not the things of the Spirit of God: for they are foolishness unto him: neither can he know them, because they are spiritually discerned.*[12]

Consider the desire that came into the heart of a young man when his father called the family together and explained the dream he had just had. Nephi so longed to know what his father knew that he declared:

> *I Nephi, was desirous also that I might see, and hear, and know of these things, by the power of the Holy Ghost, which is the gift of God unto all those who diligently seek him . . .*
>
> *For he that diligently seeketh shall find; and the mysteries of God shall be unfolded unto them, by the power of the Holy Ghost . . .*[13]
>
> *For it came to pass after I had desired to know the things that my father had seen, and believing that the Lord was able to make them known unto me, as I sat pondering in mine heart I was caught away in the Spirit of the Lord, yea, into an exceeding high mountain, which I never had before seen, and upon which I never had before set my foot.*
>
> *And the Spirit said unto me: Behold, what desirest thou?*
>
> *And I said: I desire to behold the things which my father saw.*
>
> *And the Spirit said unto me: Believest thou that thy father saw the tree of which he hath spoken?*
>
> *And I said: Yea, thou knowest that I believe all the*

---

[12] 1 Corinthians 2:14.
[13] 1 Nephi 10:17, 19.

*words of my father.*

*And when I had spoken these words, the Spirit cried with a loud voice, saying: Hosanna to the Lord, the most high God; for he is God over all the earth, yea, even above all. And blessed art thou, Nephi, because thou believest in the Son of the most high God; wherefore, thou shalt behold the things which thou hast desired.*[14]

## What About Our Day?

Has the Lord changed this manner of dealing with His children in our day? No, we are assured that He is the same forever. If there is any difference in the outpouring of the Spirit, it is because of wickedness and disbelief. A very insightful statement by Parley P. Pratt depicts some of the problems in our generation and their subsequent affect upon our intelligence and understanding.

> *. . . Men have degenerated, and greatly changed, as well as the earth. The sins, the abominations, and the many evil habits of the latter ages have added to the miseries, toils, and sufferings of human life. The idleness, extravagance, pride, covetousness, drunkenness, and other abominations, which are characteristic of the latter times, have all combined to sink mankind to the lowest state of wretchedness and degradation; while priestcraft and false doctrines have greatly tended to lull mankind to sleep, and cause them to rest infinitely short of the powers and attainments, which the ancients enjoyed, and which are alone calculated to exalt the intellectual powers of the human mind, to establish noble and generous sentiments, to enlarge the heart and to expand the soul to the utmost extent of its capacity. Witness the ancients conversing with the Great Jehovah, learning lessons from the*

---

[14] 1 Nephi 11:1-6.

*angels, and receiving instructions by the Holy Ghost, in dreams by night, and visions by day, until at length the veil is taken off, and they are permitted to gaze with wonder and admiration, upon all things past and future, yea, even to soar aloft amid unnumbered worlds, while the vast expanse of eternity stands open before them, and they contemplate the mighty works of the Great I AM, until they know as they are known and see as they are seen.*

*Compare this intelligence with the low smatterings of education and worldly wisdom which seem to satisfy the narrow mind of man in our generation . . . And having seen the two contrasted, you will be able to form some idea of the vast elevation from which man has fallen; you will also learn, how infinitely beneath his former glory and dignity he is now living; and your heart will mourn, and be exceedingly sorrowful, when you contemplate him in his low estate, and then think he is your brother; and you will be ready to exclaim, with wonder and astonishment, "Oh, man! how art thou fallen! Once thou was the favorite of heaven; thy Maker delighted to converse with thee, and angels, and the spirits of just men made perfect, were thy companions; but now thou are degraded, and brought down to a level with the beasts; yea, far beneath them, for they look with horror and affright at your vain amusements, your sports, and your drunkenness, and thus often set an example worthy of your imitation.*[15]

When will we become wise and turn from our stubbornness and cease to resist the Lord? In the particular ward where I was called to preside as Bishop, there were 95 priests. Most all of these young men were active, but there are always a few who want to exert their independence, want to make the decision to go to Priesthood on their own, do not want to be directed in

---

[15] Parley P. Pratt, *Voice of Warning*, Deseret Book, 1978, pp. 87-88.

any way. Consequently, these few took some special care and attention. One specific case I remember so well was a young man who approached me in the hallway as I was interviewing Priests.

He said, "Now, Bishop, I want to get one thing clear. I am not going on a mission."

"I've noticed that you've been interviewing all of the Priests as possible candidates to go in the mission field, and I do not want you to interview me. I have told my Bishop at home and I have told my father that I was not going on a mission, and now I want to make it implicit with you."

With inspiration I expressed, "Why, what makes you think you're worthy enough to be called on a mission?"

His face and countenance dropped.

He said, "I hadn't thought of it that way."

After getting better acquainted with this young man, he became very active and within a relatively short period of time was serving an honorable mission for the Church.

## The Promise of Knowledge

When shall we learn that what Enoch accomplished, we also can do? What his people knew, we can know! And what they were shown, we can see!

> *For thus saith the Lord—I, the Lord, am merciful and gracious unto those who fear me, and delight to honor those who serve me in righteousness and in truth unto the end.*
>
> *Great shall be their reward and eternal shall be their glory.*
>
> *And to them will I reveal all mysteries, yea, all the hidden mysteries of my kingdom from days of old, and for ages to come, will I make known unto them the good pleasure of my will concerning al things*

*pertaining to my kingdom.*

*Yea, even the wonders of eternity shall they know,
and things to come will I show them, even the things of
many generations.*

*And their wisdom shall be great, and their
understanding reach to heaven . . .*[16]

We have been invited to feast upon the fullness of the words of Christ until in the time of the Lord, we are given the keys that unlock the heavens; for the well of living water spoken of in the scriptures contains the mysteries of the Kingdom of Heaven and all knowledge. This great light and knowledge may be obtained by keeping the commandments of God. Surely, there could not be a happier people than they who walk in the light.

## Thoughts for Meditation

1.  The Holy Ghost will guide and direct us in many daily matters.

2.  When one ceases to resist the Lord, he will be blessed with greater understandings.

3.  The Lord does not desire to withhold knowledge from us.

4.  Additional light and knowledge are given when we have sufficiently prepared ourselves to receive it.

---

[16] D&C 76:5-9.

CHAPTER FIVE

# Knowledge That Saves

W hen one begins to feast upon the word of the Lord he will realize
that it is life eternal to know the Father and the Son.[1] And that to know Him
is to be like Him, to think His thoughts, to learn His ways, and finally to
have His image engraven in one's countenance.[2] Experience suggests that
these changes come naturally as one is obedient to the teachings of the
Lord and listens to the living prophets. Obedience leads to an outpouring
of the spirit of understanding—even to a knowledge of things past, present
and as they will be.

As depicted in the pervious chapter, it is the Lord's will that we
receive this knowledge, and as we prove worthy it will be shown unto us.
Then after demonstrating to the Lord that we can be trusted with added
light and knowledge,[3] much more will be given.

> . . . it is written, Eye hath not seen, nor ear heard,
> neither have entered into the heart of man, the things
> which God hath prepared for them that love him.

---

[1] See John 17:3.
[2] See Alma 5:14.
[3] See D&C 63:64.

> *But God hath revealed them unto us by his Spirit:*
> *for the Spirit searcheth all things, yea, the deep things*
> *of God.*[4]

## Sources of His Word

Where does the understanding which the Lord so generously promised come from? Alma declared that he had been commanded to stand and testify unto the people. He bore testimony concerning the source of knowledge and authority.

> *. . . Do ye not suppose that I know of these things*
> *myself? Behold, I testify unto you that I do know that*
> *these things whereof I have spoken are true. And how*
> *do ye suppose that I know of their surety?*
>
> *Behold, I say unto you they are made known unto*
> *me by the Holy Spirit of God. Behold, I have fasted and*
> *prayed many days that I might know these things of*
> *myself. And now I do know of myself that they are true;*
> *for the Lord God hath made them manifest unto me by*
> *his Holy Spirit; and this is the spirit of revelation*
> *which is in me.*[5]

Not only did Alma identify the source of his knowledge and testimony, but he went on to point out other sources of the word:

> *And moreover, I say unto you that it has thus been*
> *revealed unto me, that the words which have been*
> *spoken by our fathers are true, even so according to*
> *the spirit of prophecy which is in me, which is also by*
> *the manifestation of the Spirit of God . . .*
>
> *And now I say unto you that this is the order after*
> *which I am called, yea, to preach unto my beloved*
> *brethren, yea, and every one that dwelleth in the land;*
> *yea, to preach unto all, both old and young, both bond*

---

[4] 1 Corinthians 2:9-10.
[5] Alma 5:45-46.

> *and free; yea, I say unto you the aged, and also the middle aged, and the rising generation; yea, to cry unto them that they must repent and be born again.*[6]

Lest we err in our search for the word of the Lord, we are told in modern scripture that the arm of the Lord shall be revealed; and that the day cometh that they who will not hear the voice of the Lord, neither the voice of his servants, neither give heed to the words of the prophets and apostles, shall be cut off from among the people.[7] For thus saith the Lord:

> *What I the Lord have spoken, I have spoken, and I excuse not myself; and though the heavens and the earth pass away, my word shall not pass away, but shall all be fulfilled, whether by mine own voice or by the voice of my servants, it is the same.*[8]

> *And wo be unto him that will not hearken unto the words of Jesus, and also to them whom he hath chosen and sent among them; for whoso receiveth not the words of Jesus and the words of those whom he hath sent receiveth not him; and therefore he will not receive them at the last day.*[9]

Not only may we learn the will of the Lord by the whisperings of the Spirit, and by the voice of his servants, but we may also be taught many marvelous things by others who are appointed to impart knowledge and wisdom unto man.

> *. . . behold, I say unto you, and I would that ye should remember, that God is merciful unto all who believe on his name; therefore he desireth, in the first place, that ye should believe, yeah, even on his word.*

> *And now, he imparteth his word by angels unto men, yea, not only men but women also. Now this is not all; little children do have words given unto them many*

---

[6] Alma 5:47, 49.
[7] See D&C 1:14.
[8] D&C 1:38.
[9] 3 Nephi 28:34.

*times, which confound the wise and the learned.*[10]

*For behold, they (angels) are subject to him, to minister according to the word of his command, showing themselves unto them of strong faith and firm mind in every form of godliness.*

*And the office of their ministry is to call men unto repentance, and to fulfill and to do the work of the covenants of the Father, which he hath made unto the children of men, to prepare the way among the children of men, by declaring the word of Christ unto the chosen vessels of the Lord, that they may bear testimony of him.*[11]

By these works, the Lord God prepareth the way that all men everywhere might have faith in Christ, and through the Holy Ghost come to know all things pertaining to this earth and the inhabitants thereon. But it is asked, "If these things are true still, has the day of miracles ceased?"

*Or have angels ceased to appear unto the children of men? Or has he withheld the power of the Holy Ghost from them? Or will he, so long as time shall last, or the earth shall stand, or there shall be one man upon the face thereof to be saved?*

*Behold I say unto you, Nay; for it is by faith that miracles are wrought; and it is by faith that angels appear and minister unto men; wherefore, if these things have ceased wo be unto the children of men, for it is because of unbelief, and all is vain.*[12]

Thus we see that there are many ways in which the word of the Lord may come to the children of men.

Being in tune with His Spirit, the Holy Spirit can bring us to a knowledge of our condition before the Lord and we can, through faith,

---

[10] Alma 32:22-23.

[11] Moroni 7:30-31.

[12] Moroni 7:36-37.

know all things relative to this estate and then through strong faith and a firm mind reach beyond. If we are in tune, the will of the Lord can be made known to us. This brings two experiences to mind, each of a different nature.

When Elder Richard L. Evans was asked by the First Presidency to reorganize the BYU First, Second, and Third Stakes into three additional stakes, I had been interviewed and asked several questions pertaining to the reorganization. What a privilege it was to sit and chat with an apostle of the Lord. During a late evening orchestra rehearsal, I heard my telephone ring in an adjoining office. I answered the telephone and to my amazement the voice said:

"This is Richard L. Evans. We feel prompted by the Lord to call you to be President of the BYU Fifth Stake."

Not knowing how to respond and being somewhat in a state of shock I asked Brother Evans if I should immediately go and see him.

He said, "No, that will not be necessary, there is nothing you can do here that you cannot do where you are. Would you please let me know in the morning at 10:00 a.m. the counselors you have chosen."

Needless to say the orchestra rehearsal became meaningless and I tried to recover from the shock and think in terms of possible counselors. I went through the faculty directory, the telephone book and many other reference sources that I could find for names. During the night I prayed fervently to know the counselors the Lord would want. At about 3:00 in the morning, two names came to my mind for counselors and a third name for the clerk.

The next morning I reported to Elder Evans and he felt good about my recommendations except the second counselor was then teaching at the Institute of Religion at the University of California at Los Angeles.

He said, "How can you possibly arrange to bring this man to Provo for interviewing and sustaining without his knowing why he is coming to be interviewed, even though he will be on the BYU faculty next fall."

I told him this would not be a problem. I telephoned this prospective counselor and told him I was asking a favor. Would he meet me at the airport in Salt Lake City the next morning, even though I could not tell him the reason why.

He said, "If you were to ask me to meet you at the North Pole I would."

And he arrived on time at the airport. Elder Evans felt good about his interview and was very impressed with this type of loyalty. The stake clerk still had not been interviewed. Late Saturday afternoon I called the clerk at his office. Upon addressing him he said:

"President Goodman!"

He had not been told that I was to be the new stake president so I immediately asked what he meant by "President Goodman."

He said, "You are the new president of the BYU Fifth Stake and I am to be your stake clerk. What has taken you so long in calling me?"

Certainly this stake clerk had been in tune with the Spirit.

While serving as stake president, an extremely serious problem arose and a court had to be held in regards to a young man's membership in the Church. During the proceedings of the court most of the brethren took one position while within my heart I was unsure. Without a positive feeling about the decision to be rendered by the stake president, this particular session was adjourned. The high council was informed that when the proper promptings were given, they would again be convened.

During the week I prayed and searched for an answer to this particular problem, but the intense schedule of each day seemed to thwart any prompting from His Spirit. The following Saturday, on a calm, beautiful afternoon while pruning shrubs in the privacy of my garden, after two or three hours of communing with the Lord, I was given the proper answer to the problem. It came so forcibly and strong that several questions were asked and answered. I knew what action had to be taken. The following morning the Stake Presidency and High Council were called together and this particular experience was shared. All agreed to sustain the Stake President in the decision that the member was to be excommunicated.

Often times we may call upon the Lord, but be so busy with daily problems and pressures that He has a difficult time getting our attention for His response.

## Knowing God

Joseph Smith taught, "It is the first principle of the gospel to know for a certainty the character of God, and to know that we may converse with him as one man converses with another, and that he was once a man like us; yea, that God himself the Father of us all, dwelt on an earth, the same as Jesus Christ himself did."[13] This is a starting point from which we might gain an understanding and become fully acquainted with the mind, purposes and decrees of the great Eloheim.

> *There are but a few beings in the world who understand rightly the character of God. The great majority of mankind do not comprehend anything, either that which is past, or that which is to come, as it respects their relationship to God. They do not know, neither do they understand the nature of that relationship; and consequently they know but little above the brute beast, or more than to eat, drink and sleep. This is all man knows about God or his existence, unless it is given by the inspiration of the Almighty.*
>
> *. . . If men do not comprehend the character of God, they do not comprehend themselves. I want to go back to the beginning, and so lift your minds into a more lofty sphere and a more exalted understanding than what the human mind generally aspires to.[14]*

The Prophet then explained that there are some keys to unlock this understanding. He pointed out that notwithstanding the Apostle Peter exhorts the saints to add to their faith, virtue, knowledge, temperance, etc., yet he exhorted them to make their calling and election sure. And though

---

[13] *Teachings of the Prophet Joseph Smith*, pp. 345-46.
[14] *Teachings of the Prophet Joseph Smith*, p. 343.

they had heard an audible voice from heaven bearing testimony that Jesus was the Son of God, yet he says we have a more sure word of prophecy, "whereunto ye do well that ye take heed as unto a light shining in a dark place."

Then President Smith pointed out ". . . Wherein could they have a more sure word of prophecy than to hear the voice of God saying, This is my beloved Son."

> *Now for the secret and grand key. Though they might hear the voice of God and know that Jesus was the Son of God, this would be no evidence that their election and calling was made sure, that they had part with Christ, and were joint heirs with Him. They then would want that more sure word of prophecy, that they were sealed in the heavens and had the promise of eternal life in the kingdom of God. Then, having this promise sealed unto them, it was an anchor to the soul, sure and steadfast. Though the thunders might roll and lightnings flash, and earthquakes bellow, and war gather thick around, yet this hope and knowledge would support the soul in every hour of trial, trouble, and tribulation. Then knowledge through our Lord and Savior Jesus Christ is the grand key that unlocks the glories and mysteries of the kingdom of heaven.[15]*

## Knowing For Yourself

Speaking to the disciples the Lord explained why He spoke unto them in parables.

> *. . . it is given unto you to know the mysteries of the kingdom of heaven, but to them it is not given . . .*
>
> *Therefore speak I to them in parables: because they seeing see not; and hearing they hear not, neither do they understand.*

---

[15] *Teachings of the Prophet Joseph Smith*, p. 298.

> *And in them is fulfilled the prophecy of Esaias,*
> *which saith, By hearing ye shall hear, and shall not*
> *understand; and seeing ye shall see, and shall not*
> *perceive:*
>
> *For this people's heart is waxed gross, and their*
> *ears are dull of hearing, and their eyes they have*
> *closed; lest at any time they should see with their eyes,*
> *and hear with their ears, and should understand with*
> *their heart, and should be converted, and I should heal*
> *them.*
>
> *But blessed are your eyes, for they see: and your*
> *ears, for they hear.*[16]

If a person is past feeling, that is if he is not quickened by the Spirit through a pure heart, he may see with his natural eyes, yet not perceive God's doings; or have ears, and understand nothing. We should learn from these sayings that it is not the mortal tabernacle which discerns spiritual things, but rather the spirit that is within man.

Joseph Smith clarified this when he said, "I want to talk more of the relation of man to God. I will open your eyes . . . All things whatsoever God in his infinite wisdom has seen fit and proper to reveal to us, while we are dwelling in mortality, in regard to our mortal bodies, are revealed to us in the abstract, and independent of affinity of this mortal tabernacle, but are revealed to our spirits precisely as though we had no bodies at all; and those revelations which will save our spirits will save our bodies."[17]

Wherefore, if after we receive the word of the Lord, we do not understand it, it is because we are not spiritually awakened, and are not brought into the light.

## For What Should I Seek

Before a man can be instructed by the Spirit, he must put his life in order. For if the dominant direction of his life is not acceptable, he will, as

---

[16] Matthew 13:11, 13-16.
[17] *Teachings of the Prophet Joseph Smith*, p. 355.

Alma taught, receive the lesser portion of the word until he knows nothing concerning the mysteries of God. On the other hand, man is created with capacities

> *. . . which may be enlarged in proportion to the heed and diligence given to the light communicated from heaven to the intellect; and that the nearer man approaches perfection, the clearer are his views, and the greater his enjoyments, till he has overcome the evils of his life and lost every desire for sin; and like the ancients, arrives at that point of faith where he is wrapped in the power and glory of his Maker and is caught up to dwell with Him. But we consider that this is a station to which no man ever arrived in a moment.[18]*

In search of a model whereby we may pierce the veil placed on our understanding, let us look at some fundamental principles and prerequisites. First, it must be recognized that the Holy Ghost is the guardian of all truth and that he can, upon certain conditions, bring us to a knowledge of all secular and religious truth. Secondly, these truths are not all acquired at once, but are given unto the faithful line upon line, precept upon precept; here a little, and there a little.[19] And finally, if the recipient of these blessings does not remember that that which cometh from above is sacred, and must be spoken of with care, and by constraint of the Spirit he will find that the outpouring of the Spirit will cease.[20] For the Spirit will prove the man, whether he is able to treasure these things up in his heart and can be trusted with them.

Learning would seem to encompass at least two fundamental areas:

1.   The refinement which remakes a man in the image of his creator, and

2.   A knowledge of God's dealings with man and the wonders

---

[18] *Teachings of the Prophet Joseph Smith*, p. 51.
[19] See D&C 98:12 and D&C 128:21.
[20] See D&C 63:64.

of eternity.

The reception of guidance in both areas is based upon very specific laws and conditions. However, each in the process of purification leading to perfection will observe a consistency in the manner in which the Spirit operates. There is a rather consistent narrowing-in process. By that it is meant to suggest that as one begins, the way the Holy Spirit will work on the weightier matters, and then as he progresses through life, promptings will become increasingly more specific. In the words of a wise teacher, "There are fewer and fewer things you can do and get away with it."

If one were judged by the final standards to begin with, he would soon lose hope and would become very discouraged. So with each new milestone in the journey through mortality, there are new promptings and requirements. The way to perfection consists in living by all the light and knowledge you have acquired. You will observe that there are others living on a higher plane than you and still others beginning where you were earlier. A conscience is most at peace when ten principles are known and the person is keeping all ten. Later the Spirit will reveal new levels of spiritual living—then more is expected in order to maintain the same tranquility. We can be assured of this, however, the way becomes narrower and narrower, until the view becomes clearer and enjoyments greater, until all disposition to do evil is lost.[21]

## A Model for Learning

Since there are specific principles of perfection and knowledge which all must acquire in mortality, it seems reasonable to conclude that some ways are better than others for learning them. And although the Lord deals with each individually, there are some commonalities about life which suggest a plan. A guide to bring us safely through.

One of the greatest difficulties to overcome as we begin this life is the lack of vision due to the veil which was placed over the mind of our understanding at birth. Yet when we narrow down that which is really important, it is mostly unseen. The distant past and the future exist only in

---

[21] See Mosiah 5:2.

the mind. And when without vision, we pretend that the unseen is like the seen, many erroneous concepts fill our minds. It is only when we escape the physical that truth can be discerned.

Through the physical body, much experience passes which is useful and necessary. For our flesh could not become refined and patterned after the image of the Lord without the experiences of this life. However, it is soon observed that the body is helpless to refine itself. It must be subjected to a greater law. We spend so much time responding to the physical senses, however, that we overlook the exciting and sanctifying realm just beyond our mortal sight.

Just as a man may build up a reservoir of knowledge by carefully classifying each phenomenon and fact of the natural world into laws and theories, he may also apply the same logic to the spiritual realm. So little effort, though, is spent with the latter aspects of learning that it is no wonder we become spiritual pygmies. In order to develop a full awareness of the world of the spirit, we must look within. There one will discover a whole new body of knowledge. It is within this realm that the mysteries of God are found.

> *Knowledge which is beyond human compre-*
> *hension is usually classified as a mystery. Yet, when a*
> *thing is understood it is no longer a mystery. In the*
> *eternal sense there are no mysteries; all things are*
> *known to and understood by Deity, and there shall be*
> *no mysteries among exalted beings, for they too shall*
> *know all things. Accordingly, some matters of doctrine,*
> *philosophy, or science may be a mystery to one person*
> *and not to another.*[22]

How may we then learn these mysteries that they may become a part of our own awareness? In the first place they can only be learned by the Spirit. This is not a formidable problem though. Each of us has a spirit and experiences spiritual phenomena as a part of our consciousness. There is in the consciousness of all those who are not trapped in gross wickedness

---

[22] Bruce R. McConkie, *Mormon Doctrine* (1st Edition), Mysteries, p. 473.

an awareness of those things which come through the physical senses and things which rather obviously have their origin within.

A perceptive teacher observed that nearly everyone has what is called flashes of insight. Ideas that just pop into the mind. They cannot be accounted for, because nothing was heard nor were any of the other physical senses involved. If people were as willing to think carefully about those kinds of phenomena as they are to think about those that come through the body, it would be discovered that there are some regularities about spiritual experiences. Just as there are causes and consequences in the natural world, there are also predictable outcomes within the spiritual realm.

The question is thought, how may we lay hold upon these things? The Lord declared some prerequisites:

> *Verily, thus saith the Lord: It shall come to pass that every soul who forsaketh his sins and cometh unto me, and calleth on my name, and obeyeth my voice, and keepeth my commandments, shall see my face and know that I am;*
>
> *And that I am the true light that lighteth every man that cometh into the world.*[23]

By doing these things we place ourselves in a position where his Spirit may be poured out upon us. If you really want to become a spiritual giant, concentrate on the world within. How? Meditation. President McKay said that meditation is the language of the soul and that inspiration does not come under the pressure of your appointment; but rather, during the quiet hours of your meditation.

Solomon once said about man, "As he thinketh in his heart, so is he."[24]

What does that suggest about the many who do not take the time to think and to meditate? We nourish the body several times daily, but often lack the wisdom to see the spirit's needs. Have we not been admonished

---

[23] D&C 93:1-2.
[24] Proverbs 23:7.

that there is a constant need to nourish both the body and the spirit?

> *Draw near unto me and I will draw near unto you;*
> *seek me diligently and ye shall find me; ask, and ye*
> *shall receive; knock, and it shall be opened unto*
> *you . . .*

> *Behold, that which you hear is the voice of one*
> *crying in the wilderness—in the wilderness, because*
> *you cannot see him—my voice, because my voice is*
> *Spirit; my Spirit is truth; truth abideth and hath no*
> *end; and if it be in you it shall abound.*

> *And if your eye be single to my glory, your whole*
> *bodies shall be filled with light, and there shall be no*
> *darkness in you; and that body which is filled with light*
> *comprehendeth all things.*[25]

We cannot see out of our bodies through our physical eyes. If we are to see at all, it is through the light of the eyes of our spirit. If we cannot see in this manner, then we can *feel* the presence of the Spirit. When we are "past feeling," then we are in a condition known as being spiritually dead.[26]

> *Therefore, sanctify yourselves that you minds*
> *become single to God, and the days will come that you*
> *shall see him; for he will unveil his fact unto you . . .*

> *. . . Prepare yourselves, and sanctify yourselves;*
> *yea, purify your hearts, and cleanse your hands and*
> *your feet before me, that I may make you clean.*[27]

> *Look unto me in every thought; doubt not, fear*
> *not.*[28]

"And this is life eternal, that they might know thee the only true God, and Jesus Christ, whom thou has sent" (John 17:3). It is one thing to know about God; to have information relative to his character, perfection, and

---

[25] D&C 88:63, 66-67.
[26] 1 Nephi 17:45.
[27] D&C 88:68, 74.
[28] D&C 6:36.

attributes; and to know what he has done and is doing for men and all created things. But it is quite another thing to know God in the real, full, and accurate sense of the word. We do not know the Lord unless and until we think what he thinks, say what he says, and experience what he experiences. In other words, we know God when we become like him; for arriving at this condition, we will have found the knowledge that saves. Even the key to eternal life.

## Thoughts for Meditation

1. Obedience leads to an outpouring of the spirit of understanding.

2. It is not the mortal tabernacle which discerns spiritual things, but rather the spirit that is within man.

3. There are several sources of knowledge. I should know what they are and learn how to take advantage of them.

4. Before one can be instructed by the Spirit, he must put his own life in order.

5. It is important that I learn to "feel His word."

## Chapter Six

# The Role of Adversity in Our Lives

$O$ne cannot develop a full understanding and sensitivity to his feelings and emotions without mortal experience. An integral part of the plan includes all connotations associated with the law of the opposites. A desire to be obedient is developed as we learn that for every choice there is a consequence. And that for every wrong choice there is an accompanying sorrow and for every right choice, a blessing.

But as shall be pointed out, not all tribulations are a result of disobedience. Some things were meant to be a natural part of this telestial level of existence. It is our task to learn when we are being chastened and when we are being taught from on high. Then gain knowledge from both. The Lord declared to Moroni:

> . . . *if men come unto me I will show unto them their weakness. I give men weakness that they may be humble; and my grace is sufficient for all men that humble themselves before me; for if they humble themselves before me, and have faith in me, then will I make weak things become strong unto them.*[1]

If we are wise, we will reflect humbly upon those things which the Lord seeth fit to inflict upon us, and we will develop a wholesome attitude

---

[1] Ether 12:27.

about that which rather apparently comes from Him for our good. Not even the Son of Man could obtain a fullness without these mellowing influences. Paul wrote to the Hebrews saying:

> *Though he were a Son, yet learned he obedience*
> *by the things which he suffered;*
>
> *And being made perfect, he became the author of*
> *eternal salvation unto all them that obey him.*[2]

One paradox which has always seemed peculiar is that after overcoming the world we arrive at a condition where we are finally worthy enough to be persecuted. Reflection upon this phenomenon, though, suggests that until we overcome by faith, we are not sons and daughters of God.

And if we are not His, then Satan laith claim upon our souls. Surely, the adversary would not persecute his own. In the end, not being a good shepherd, he will abandon those who have obeyed his voice.

Some examples of those who did not escape the trials of this life by reason of their great works include:

1.  Abinadi—who, after being called to bear testimony against King Noah and his priests, was burned to death.

2.  Nephi—who, because of an undeviating course, was repeatedly bound and beaten by his brothers.

3.  Noah—How would you like to spend a lifetime building a boat where there was no water, even in the evening when you are really tired, and preach the gospel for 120 years where practically no one would listen? Then use the boat only once!

4.  Christ's Apostles—All suffered violent deaths, except John.

5.  Joseph Smith—Whose whole life was beset with trials and ended with his violent death.

---

[2] Hebrews 5:8-9.

## Some Reflections

Two of the most penetrating questions asked of me, while serving as a bishop, were these:

1. "Bishop, why did the Spirit of the Lord leave me? I didn't break any commandments."

2. "If the Lord really loved me, why did he let that happen?"

Understanding, in time, will come to those who bear all things patiently. Know this, these questions are relevant. Strength becomes stronger and solidified by the withdrawal of the Lord's Spirit for a testing purpose. It is because he loves us that adversity comes. Let us forsake the false notion that problems come only by reason of transgression. President Brigham Young is quoted as making the observation that the Prophet was more perfect in 38 years, with the severe tribulation through which he passed, than he would have been in a thousand years without it.

## Scriptural Affirmation

Blessings are promised those who in this life are called upon to suffer for the Lord's cause. Jesus taught in the Sermon on the Mount:

> *Blessed are they which are persecuted for righteousness' sake: for theirs is the kingdom of heaven.*
>
> *Blessed are ye, when men shall revile you, and persecute you, and shall say all manner of evil against you falsely, for my sake.*
>
> *Rejoice, and be exceeding glad: for great is your reward in heaven: for so persecuted they the prophets which were before you.*[3]

The apostle John quoted Jesus when he wrote:

> *In the world ye shall have tribulation: but be of*

---

[3] Matthew 5:10-12.

*good cheer; I have overcome the world.*[4]

In this dispensation Joseph Smith received a revelation wherein the Lord promised that:

> *All they who suffer persecution for my name, and endure in faith, though they are called to lay down their lives for my sake yet shall they partake of all this glory.*
>
> *Wherefore, fear not even unto death; for in this world your joy is not full, but in me your joy is full.*
>
> *. . . Seek the face of the Lord always, that in patience ye may possess your souls, and ye shall have eternal life.*[5]

Only after one has spent considerable effort wrestling with his own problems will he have the patience, concern and understanding to help others. If these lessons could have been learned in any other way or acquired in fewer years, it is doubtful that the Lord would have planned to allow us so much time here on the earth.

From the echoes of the past comes the petition, "Is there no other way?" And the response, "There is no other way!" Even if all men were to come unto the Lord and enter into his everlasting covenants, adversity would still be with us. The Prophet Joseph put this principle into these words, "Men have to suffer that they may come upon Mount Zion and be exalted above the Heavens."[6]

## Strength and Struggle

I remember once after a particularly good Sunday School class one of the class members came up and remarked, "I wish I were like you and didn't have any problems." After thinking that over a while, I decided to send her a copy of a poem by Harry Kemp, entitled "A Prayer."

---

[4] John 16:33.
[5] D&C 101:35, 36, and 38.
[6] *History of the Church*, 5:556.

I kneel not now to pray that Thou
Make white one single sin
I only kneel to thank thee, Lord
For what I have not been—

For deeds which sprouted in my heart
But ne'er to bloom were brought,
For monstrous vices which I slew
In the shambles of my thought—

Dark seeds the world has never guessed,
By Hell and passion bred,
Which never grew beyond the bud
That cankered in my head.

Some said I was a righteous man—
Poor fools! The gallows tree
If thou hadst let one foot to slip
Had grown a limb for me.

I have thought many times that no man knows the weight of another's burdens. Life today carries with it such trials that it is marvelous the way people carry the burdens they do have to bear. In many ways the psychological and mental pressures of our generation are as trying as were the physical privations of our forefathers. Nevertheless, the strength to overcome is available to us from the same source that brought them through. And when someone encounters difficulties, and they are resolved, the power attained from them will be a part of the person ever after.

> . . . *we glory in tribulations also: knowing that*
> *tribulation worketh patience:*
>
> *and patience, experience; and experience hope:*[7]

Let us then thank the Lord for our inevitable adversities. It is through these trying experiences that power comes, confidence is built, and every step forward a lasting lesson. Phillip Brooks is quoted as saying, "that you may look through the streets of heaven, asking each how he came there,

---

[7] Romans 5:3-4.

and you will look in vain everywhere for a man morally or spiritually strong, whose strength did not come to him in struggle . . . There is no exception anywhere. There is no time in life when opportunity, the chance to be and do, gathers so richly about the soul as when it has to suffer. Then everything depends on whether the man turns to the lower or the higher helps. If he resorts to mere expedients and tricks, the opportunity is lost. He comes out no richer nor greater; nay, he comes out harder, poorer, smaller for his pain. But, if he turns to God, the hour of suffering is the turning hour of his life."

## The Refiner's Fire

These struggles provide the means whereby unregenerated man might be refined and purified. Through this process we are reborn into a newness of life. The "old man"[8] is no more, and the new man is called the son of God.

> *Behold, what manner of love the Father hath bestowed upon us, that we should be called the sons of God: therefore the world knoweth us not, because it knew him not.*
>
> *Beloved, now are we the sons of God, and it doth not yet appear what we shall be: but we know that, when he shall appear, we shall be like him; for we shall see him as he is.*
>
> *And every man that hath this hope in him purifieth himself, even as he is pure.*[9]

We can be assured that he who brought us forth, knoweth our disposition and our every need. The refinement required is different for each of his children. The ultimate goal is the same. Therefore,

> *. . . despise not the chastening of the Lord; neither be weary of his correction;*
>
> *For whom the Lord loveth he correcteth; even as*

---

[8] Romans 6:6.
[9] 1 John 3:1-3.

*a father the son in whom he delighteth.*[10]

Every soul who ultimately gains exaltation will be tried to the uttermost. If there is any weakness in our character, we can be assured that the Lord will test us at that spot. Then as Joseph Smith declared, When the Lord has thoroughly proved us and found that we are determined to serve Him at all hazards, then we will find ourselves pure and our calling and election made sure.[11]

## A Reassurance

One of the most enlightening scriptures indicating the Lord's plan for refining us is found in the Doctrine and Covenants. This reassurance should help us to bear whatever is necessary until answers come.

*Be thou humble; and the Lord thy God shall lead thee by the hand, and give thee answer to thy prayers.*[12]

Then the Lord gave counsel to the first quorum of Twelve Apostles which would be worthwhile for all of us to ponder; for the process is the same today.

*. . . After their temptations and much tribulation, behold, I, the Lord, will feel after them, and if they harden not their hearts, and stiffen not their necks against me, they shall be converted, and I will heal them.*[13]

Speaking of the Lord's power to bring us through the trials of the latter days and to keep us close to him, Paul wrote:

*Who shall separate us from the love of Christ? shall tribulation, or distress, or persecution, or famine, or nakedness, or peril, or sword?*

*As it is written, For thy sake we are killed all the*

---

[10] Proverbs 3:11-12, and Hebrews 12:5-7.
[11] See *Teachings of the Prophet Joseph Smith*, p. 150.
[12] D&C 112:10.
[13] D&C 112:13.

> *day long; we are accounted as sheep for the slaughter.*
>
> *Nay, in all these things we are more than conquerors through him that loved us.*
>
> *For I am persuaded that neither death, nor life, nor angels, nor principalities, nor powers, nor things present, nor things to come,*
>
> *Nor height, nor depth, nor any other creature, shall be able to separate us from the love of God, which is in Christ Jesus our Lord.[14]*

Surely, His children shall not be overcome, if they will but listen to the whisperings of the Spirit and contemplate the great love which He showers upon all those who believe. Though earth and hell shall combine against us, the reward only becomes greater for those who endure.

Nevertheless, Satan cannot prevail except we succumb to his lies and lose our source of strength and inner peace. Paul wrote to the Corinthians:

> *We are troubled on every side, yet not distressed; we are perplexed, but not in despair;*
>
> *Persecuted, but not forsaken; cast down, but not destroyed;[15]*

Peter gave us cause for additional hope and encouragement when he wrote:

> *. . . if ye suffer for righteousness' sake, happy are ye: and be not afraid of their terror, neither be troubled;*
>
> *But sanctify the Lord God in your hearts: and be ready always to give an answer to every man that asketh you a reason of the hope that is in you with meekness and fear (reverence).[16]*

---

[14] Romans 8:35-39.
[15] 2 Corinthians 4:8-9.
[16] 1 Peter 3:14-15.

## Comfort from Our Hymns

Some of the sweetest words of comfort concerning the Lord's manner of refining his children come from the inspired verses of the hymns we sing. Read slowly the following few examples, reflecting upon the feelings they evoke. Then when you approach worship services in the future, lift your voice in prayer and supplication upon the Lord with greater meaning.

### HOW FIRM A FOUNDATION

Fear not, I am with thee; oh, be not dismayed,
For I am thy God and will still give thee aid.
I'll strengthen thee, help thee, and cause thee to stand,
Upheld by my righteous, omnipotent hand.

When through the deep waters I call thee to go,
The rivers of sorrow shall not thee o'er flow
For I will be with thee, thy troubles to bless,
And sanctify to thee thy deepest distress.

When through fiery trials thy pathway shall lie,
My grace, all sufficient, shall be thy supply.
The flame shall not hurt thee; I only design
Thy dross to consume and thy gold to refine.[17]

### GOD MOVES IN A MYSTERIOUS WAY

God moves in a mysterious way
His wonders to perform;
He plants his footsteps in the sea
And rides upon the storm.

Ye fearful Saints, fresh courage take;
The clouds ye so much dread
Are big with mercy and shall break
In blessings on your head.

---

[17] How Firm A Foundation, *Hymns*, 1985, #85.

His purposes will ripen fast,
Unfolding ever hour;
The bud may have a bitter taste,
But sweet will be the flower.

Blind unbelief is sure to err
And scan his works in vain;
God is his own interpreter,
And he will make it plain.[18]

### LEAD KINDLY LIGHT

Lead kindly light, amid th' encircling gloom;
Lead thou me on!
The night is dark, and I am far from home;
Lead thou me on!
Keep thou my feet; I do not ask to see
The distant scene—one step enough for me.

I was not ever thus, nor pray'd that thou
Shouldst lead me on.
I loved to choose and see my path; but now,
Lead thou me on!
I loved the garish day, and, spite of fears,
Pride ruled my will. Remember not past years.

So long thy power hath blest me, sure it still
Will lead me on
O'er moor and fen, o'er crag and torrent, til
The night is gone.
And with the morn those angel faces smile,
Which I have loved long since, and lost a-while![19]

### MASTER THE TEMPEST IS RAGING

Master, the tempest is raging!
The billows are tossing high!

---

[18] God Moves In A Mysterious Way, *Hymns,* 1985, #285.
[19] Lead Kindly Light, *Hymns*, 1985, #97.

The sky is o'er-shadowed with blackness.
No shelter or help is nigh.
Carest thou not that we perish?
How canst thou lie asleep
When each moment so madly is threatening
A grave in the angry deep?

Master, with anguish of spirit
I bow in my grief today.
The depths of my sad heart are troubled.
Oh, waken and save, I pray!
Torrents of sin and of anguish
Sweep o'er my sinking soul,
And I perish! I perish! dear Master.
Oh, hasten and take control!

Master, the terror is over.
The elements sweetly rest.
Earth's sun in the calm lake is mirrored,
And heaven's within my breast.
Linger, Oh blessed Redeemer!
Leave me alone no more,
And with joy I shall make the blest harbor
And rest on the blissful shore.[20]

Look at it this way, if a man has entered into all of the new and everlasting covenants and is seeking with all the energy of his soul to keep the commandments, the only chance Satan has of stealing away his soul is to keep him alive. Once beyond this sphere he will no longer have such a powerful influence over him.

## Then, Why Should We Fear?

Let us press forward, feasting upon the pleasing word of Christ, giving thanks daily for the privilege of being here, being grateful for the experiences which will make us strong, and continue in the peace which the

---

[20] Master, the Tempest is Raging, *Hymns,* 1985, #105.

Lord promised he would leave with us,[21] knowing that all these things shall give us experience, and shall be for our good.[22]

Orson F. Whitney, expressed how needful these basic laws of spiritual growth are to each of us in his magnificent poem, *The Mount and the Vale.*

There's a mountain named Stern Justice
Tall and towering, gloomy, grand.
Frowning over a vale called Mercy
Loveliest in all the land.

Great and mighty is the mountain
But its snowy crags are cold
And in vain the sunlight lingers
On the summit proud and bold.

There is warmth within the valley
And I love to wander there
Mid the fountains and the flowers
Breathing fragrance on the air.

Much I love the solemn mountain
It doth meet my somber mood
When amid the muttering thunders
O'er my soul the storm clouds brood.

But when tears like rain have fallen
From the fountains of my woe
And my soul has lost its fierceness
Straight unto the vale I go.

When the landscape gently smiling
O'er my heart pours healing balm
And as oil on troubled waters
Brings from out its storm a calm.

Yes, I love both Vale and Mountain

---

[21] See John 14:27.
[22] See D&C 122:7.

> Ne'er from either would I part
> Each unto my life is needful
> Both are dear unto my heart.
>
> For the smiling vale doth soften
> All the rugged steep make sad
> And from icy rocks meander
> Rills that make the valley glad.[23]

## The Treasure in Adversity

. . . Some of the lowliest walks in life, the paths which lead into the deepest valleys of sorrow and up to the most rugged steeps of adversity, are the ones which, if a man travel in, will best accomplish the object of his existence in this world . . . The conditions which place men where they may always walk on the unbroken plain of prosperity and seek for nothing but their own pleasure, are not the best within the gift of God. For in such circumstances men soon drop into a position analogous to the stagnant pool; while those who have to contend with difficulties, brave dangers, endure disappointments, struggle with sorrows, eat the bread of adversity and drink the water of affliction, develop a moral and spiritual strength, together with a purity of life and character, unknown to the heirs of ease and wealth and pleasure. With the English bard, therefore, I believe: Sweet are the uses of adversity![24]

## Thoughts for Meditation

1.  Understanding will come in time to those who bear all things patiently.

2.  Forsake the false notion that problems come only by reason of transgression.

3.  The ability to really help others comes only after we have wrestled with and overcome our own weaknesses.

---

[23] Orson F. Whitney, *The Mountain and The Vale.*
[24] B. H. Roberts, *Man's Relationship to Deity*, pp. 280-90.

4. If we completely humble ourselves, the Lord will give us answers to our prayers.

5. Even the greatest of adversity, when overcome, will best fulfill the purpose of our existence in this world.

6. Don't pray that these trials be totally taken from you, but rather, that you may have the power to overcome them.

CHAPTER SEVEN

# Becoming His Sons and His Daughters

P ersons who have the experience of the Spirit withdrawing without transgression find a new principle in the refining process. After feasting upon the words of the Lord and finding the new knowledge pleasing, there comes a testing period—a trial of faith. So often we never arrive at this more positive learning experience, because all we have experienced is the discouragement felt when the Holy Spirit withdraws because of transgression. Then after much sorrow and repentance the Spirit returns to sustain and succor.

The time must eventually come when, like the Lord, we too put all things under our feet. Strength to accomplish this comes as we learn and are subsequently tested. These proving periods, if successfully borne, lead to higher spiritual plateaus. For as we learned earlier, the Lord proveth and chasteneth every son whom he receiveth.[1]

An important lesson of patience must be learned early, however, in order to understand the refiner's fire and not be discouraged. An experience of some years ago may provide insight into the Lord's patience in dealing with his children while leading them back to the Father.

---

[1] See Hebrews 12:5-8.

While walking home one summer afternoon, the Spirit impressed upon my soul the importance of being patient with ourselves in the refining process. Perfection is not achieved in a single day nor in a single effort. For most of us it is a lifelong process with growth being more rapid at some periods than another. In marveling about the long-suffering kindness of the Lord a simple analogy came to my mind.

The Spirit prompted, "When you were teaching your son Jon Thomas to walk, how many times did you spank him because he could not walk across the room the first day."

Nonsense I thought, we were so excited about each additional step that we were all laughing and enjoying the new experience.

"This is how the Lord feels. Each new spiritual step is greeted with such joy that no thought is given to punishment because you cannot run spiritually. First come spiritual baby steps."

The prompting came again, "Did you punish your son because he could not run around the house in one month?"

"No! Again we were satisfied with his progress and proud of him," I thought.

"Then, remember that there is joy in heaven over every lesson learned. It was expected to take a lifetime. First, you spiritually walk as a child, by faith. Then, seeing, your steps become more sure; and finally, when quickened by a fullness, faith is swallowed up in knowledge—then your spiritual pace will quicken."

This refining and learning process is related to the "narrowing-in process" referred to earlier. Knowledge is gained at the same pace we overcome and refine our bodies. How important it is to keep perspective, lest the adversary catch us in a weak moment and convince us we cannot win the race. The prize does not necessarily go to the swift, nor is there a greater reward for those, who hearing the word, begin sooner than others. It is required only that the labor be earnest, once begun.

*For the kingdom of heaven is like unto a man that*
*is an householder, which went out early in the morning*

*to hire labourers into his vineyard.*

*And when he had agreed with the labourers for a penny a day, he sent them into his vineyard.*[2]

*During the day others were observed idle and were sent into the vineyard, saying "whatever is right I will give you."*[3]

*And about the eleventh hour he went out, and found others standing idle, and saith unto them, Why stand ye here all the day Idle?*

*They say unto him, Because no man hath hired us. He saith unto them, Go ye also into the vineyard; . . .*[4]

Now when evening came the Lord of the vineyard commanded his steward to call the labourers together and "give them their hire, beginning from the last to the first." When those who were hired last came forth each received a penny.[5]

When the first came for their wages they supposed that they would receive more, but they likewise received a penny. And when they received it they began to murmur and complain because they, who had borne the heat of the day, were made equal with those who worked but an hour.[6]

So it is in the kingdom. Many will enter into the covenant after others have labored long in the vineyard. But those who love the Lord and know his purposes find joy in any soul that cometh into the fold and will not feel in their hearts to murmur because the fullness is promised to another who labored less. Surely the Lord will say unto them, "Blessed are they that rejoice when Zion prospers and who labor diligently to prepare the kingdom for the coming of the bridegroom."

---

[2] Matthew 20:1-2.
[3] Matthew 20:4.
[4] Matthew 20:6-7.
[5] Matthew 20:8-9.
[6] See Matthew 20:10-12.

## The Power to Bind Satan

It was intended that we be tried and proven in this estate. The life of each must be weighed in the balance and not found lacking. And since we are his whom we list to obey, all would do well to seek assurance that the voice to which we surrender obedience is the voice of the Good Shepherd and not the evil one.

> *For the kingdom of the devil must shake, and they which belong to it must needs be stirred up unto repentance, or the devil will grasp them with his everlasting chains, and they be stirred up to anger, and perish;*
>
> *For behold, at that day shall he rage in the hearts of the children of men, and stir them up to anger against that which is good.*
>
> *And others will he pacify, and lull away into carnal security, that they will say: All is well in Zion; yea, Zion prospereth, all is well—and thus the devil cheateth their souls, and leadeth them away carefully down to hell.*
>
> *And behold, others he flattereth away, and telleth them there is no hell; and he saith unto them: I am no devil, for there is none—and thus he whispereth in their ears, until he grasps them with his awful chains, from whence there is no deliverance.[7]*
>
> *Therefore, wo be unto him that is at ease in Zion! . . .*
>
> *Yea, wo be unto him that hearkeneth unto the precepts of men, and denieth the power of God, and the gift of the Holy Ghost! . . .*
>
> *And in fine, wo unto all those who tremble, and are angry because of the truth of God! For behold, he*

---

[7] 2 Nephi 28:19-22.

*that is built upon the rock receiveth it with gladness.*[8]

Thus we see that except the children of men hearken unto the voice of the Lord and give ear unto His counsels, the adversary may lay claim upon their souls. Yet, if we call upon God with all the energy of our hearts, Satan may be bound and have no more place in us. Moses provided the key to this power in his description of when he was tempted by Satan after the Lord had showed him the world and the ends thereof. Satan came to him saying:

> *. . . Moses, son of man, worship me.*
>
> *And it came to pass that Moses looked upon Satan and said: Who art thou? For behold, I am a son of God, in the similitude of his Only Begotten; and where is thy glory, that I should worship thee? . . .*
>
> *Blessed be the name of my God, for his Spirit hath not altogether withdrawn from me, or else where is thy glory, for it is darkness unto me? . . .*
>
> *Get thee hence, Satan; deceive me not. . . .*[9]

What seems significant is that Satan did not leave when commanded, whereupon Moses commanded again.

> *And now, when Moses had said these words, Satan cried with a loud voice, and ranted upon the earth, and commanded, saying: I am the Only Begotten, worship me.*
>
> *And it came to pass that Moses began to fear exceedingly; and as he began to fear, he saw the bitterness of hell. Nevertheless, calling upon God, he received strength, and he commanded, saying: Depart from me, Satan, for this one God only will I worship, which is the God of glory.*
>
> *And now Satan began to tremble, and the earth shook; and Moses received strength, and called upon*

---

[8] 2 Nephi 28:24, 26, 28.
[9] Moses 1:12, 13, 15, 16.

*God, saying:* In the name of the Only Begotten, depart hence, Satan! *(Emphasis ours)*

*And it came to pass that Satan cried with a loud voice, with weeping, and wailing, and gnashing of teeth; and he departed hence, even from the presence of Moses, that he beheld him not.*

*And now of this thing Moses bore record; but because of wickedness it is not had among the children of men.*[10]

Recently a young elder in the Church called about 1:00 a.m. in regards to the traumatic condition of one of the ward members. He indicated over the telephone that she seemed to be possessed of Satan. She had been swimming during the afternoon and ever since the swim had seemed to be possessed. He did not know if her condition was the result of a tumor that she had previously had or whether there was some satanic influence preying upon her. Since this young man was unable to locate the bishop he was instructed to call the first counselor and asked him to go assist in administering to this sister.

When the elders arrived, the stricken sister ridiculed them and wanted to know who they were. They indicated that they were representing the bishopric and that they were there to administer to her, at the suggestion of the Stake President. She scoffed, laughed and wanted to know by what authority. He told her by the authority of Jesus Christ and the Melchizedek Priesthood. She again laughed. She resisted the administration until they were forced to hold her still. As soon as the consecrated oil was administered to the crown of her head she seemed to relax and allowed them to proceed. During the administration this fine counselor thought he would bless her for her good health, but he was prompted to cast Satan from her very being. As soon as this was done the young lady was restored to her normal state. After the administration was completed she said, "Now I know who you are and I recognize by what authority you come." Truly this sister had been possessed by Satan, and Satan had been rebuked.

---

[10] Moses 1:19-23.

To those who have grasped the iron rod, power is given whereby in the name of the Lord Jesus Christ, Satan may be bound. Even to all children of the covenant, who are pure in heart, is this power given. This key is yours so that the cunning plans and snares of the devil might not be more than you can bear. You can put all things under your feet—through Him who overcame the world.[11]

## Blessed are the Pure in Heart

Those who love the Lord and keep His commandments, have as their objective the cleansing, purifying, and sanctifying of their own souls. These are they who have bridled their passions, put off the natural man and become saints through the atonement;[12] who have been born again; becoming the sons and daughters of Christ;[13] who shall see God.[14]

> *Therefore, sanctify yourselves that your minds become single to God, and the days will come that you shall see him, for he will unveil his face unto you . . .*
>
> *. . . Yea, purify your hearts, and cleanse your hands and feet before me, that I may make you clean.[15]*

All who will subdue the natural man shall not be found asleep, and shall abide the day of the Lord's coming; for they shall be purified even as he is pure.[16]

> *Wherefore, my beloved brethren, pray unto the Father with all the energy of heart, that ye may be filled with this love, which he hath bestowed upon all who are true followers of his Son, Jesus Christ; that ye may become the sons of God; that when he shall appear we shall be like him, for we shall see him as he is; that we may have this hope; that we may be purified*

---

[11] See John 16:33.

[12] See Mosiah 3:19.

[13] See Mosiah 5:7.

[14] See Matthew 5:8 and D&C 93:1.

[15] D&C 88:68, 74.

[16] See D&C 35, 21.

*even as he is pure.*[17]

His ministerings unto us shall not cease so long as we are "of strong faith and a firm mind in every form of godliness."[18]

> *O all ye that are pure in heart, lift up your heads*
> *and receive the pleasing word of God, and feast upon*
> *his love; for ye may, if your minds are firm, forever.*[19]

After these changes begin to occur in our hearts, and we seek to save ourselves from "this untoward generation,"[20] King Benjamin tells us that the Spirit of the Lord Omnipotent can "wrought a mighty change in us, or in our hearts, that we will have no more disposition to do evil, but to do good continually,"[21] Eventually, in this life, the hearts of the Saints generally will be pure, for Zion is to be redeemed by the pure in heart.

> For I will raise up unto myself a pure people, that will serve me in righteousness.[22]

### Hearkening Unto Counsel

Questions are frequently asked as to why our leaders do not speak to the membership of the Church saying, "Thus saith the Lord God." Would this not, they say, clarify when they speak the will of the Lord unto the people and when general counsel is being given. We would do well to understand that it is not a wise servant who must be commanded in all things. In this there is no reward.[23]

Refinement comes as we hearken to the counsel of the Lord and to the counsel of His servants. Herein can a man please God, by listening to the voice of the Spirit within. For it will teach you all things whatsoever you should do.[24] In this there is no need for compulsion.

---

[17] Moroni 7:48.
[18] Moroni 7:30.
[19] Jacob 3:2.
[20] D&C 36:6.
[21] Mosiah 5:2.
[22] D&C 100:16.
[23] See D&C 58:26.
[24] See 2 Nephi 32:2-6.

Consider how mixed up Abraham would have been had he tried to unscramble the logic of sacrificing his son Isaac. When we are in tune with the Spirit and heeding the promptings there is no need for questioning the wisdom of the matter.

On the day the Church was organized, the Lord said this: "Wherefore, meaning the Church"—and that was addressed not just to the few on that day, but to all who have been or who will be members of this Church—"thou shall give heed unto all his words and commandments which he shall give unto you as he receiveth them, walking in all holiness before me;

> *For his word (meaning the president of the Church) ye shall receive, as if from mine own mouth, in all patience and faith.*[25]

Now note the promise if we will be thus obedient to seek counsel and to accept counsel form the proper channels:

> *For by doing these things the gates of hell shall not prevail against you; yea, and the Lord God will disperse the powers of darkness from before you, and cause the heavens to shake for your good and in his name's glory.*[26]

To you Latter-day Saints everywhere, that promise will be yours if you will follow the leadership the Lord has placed within the Church, giving heed to their counsel in patience and faith.[27]

If we accept counsel thoughtfully, feeling that it is the same as though we heard the phrase, "Thus saith the Lord," we would be found standing in Holy Places.

These will "be washed and cleansed from all their sins," and are they "who overcome by faith, and are sealed by the Holy Spirit of Promise, which the Father sheds forth upon all those who are just and true."

---

[25] D&C 21:4-5.

[26] D&C 21:6

[27] See Harold B. Lee, The Way to Eternal Life, *The Ensign,* Vol. I, No. II. November 1971, pp. 11-12.

*They are they who are the church of the Firstborn.*

*They are they into whose hands the Father has given all things—*

*They are they who are priests and kings, who have (as rightful heirs) received of his fullness, and of his glory; . . .*

*Wherefore, as it is written, they are gods, even sons of God—*

*Wherefore all things are theirs, whether life or death, or things present, or things to come, all are theirs and they are Christ's, and Christ is Gods' . . .*

*These shall dwell in the presence of God and his Christ forever and ever.*[28]

## His Sons and Daughters are Heirs

Now these are they who the Father has given unto the Son. These are the ones who have overcome by faith. The Lord said unto Alma:

*. . . Marvel not that all mankind, yea, men and women, all nations, kindreds, tongues and people, must be born again; yea, born of God, changed from their carnal and fallen state, to a state of righteousness, being redeemed of God, becoming his sons and daughters;*

*And thus they become new creatures; and unless they do this, they can in nowise inherit the kingdom of God.*[29]

Paul taught that if we live after the flesh we shall die: but if we through the Spirit mortify the deeds of the body, we shall live. For those who are continually led by the Spirit of God, which is to say by the voice of His counsels, are the sons and daughters of God. Hath not the Spirit born

---

[28] D&C 76:52-56, 58-59, 62.
[29] Mosiah 27:25-26.

witness to our spirit that we are the children of God.[30]

> *And if children, then heirs; heirs of God, and*
> *joint-heirs with Christ; if so be that we suffer with him,*
> *that we may be also glorified together.*[31]

In his famous King Follett Sermon, speaking of those who "Shall be heirs of god and joint-heirs with Jesus Christ," the Prophet asked what their glory should be, then answering his own query, he described joint-heirship as inheriting "the same power, the same glory and the same exaltation, until you arrive at the station of a God and ascend the throne of eternal power, the same as those who have gone before.[32]

A joint heir is one who inherits equally with all other heirs including the Chief Heir who is the Son. Each joint-heir has an equal and an undivided portion of the whole of everything. If one knows all things, so do all others. If one has all power, so do all those how inherit jointly with him. If the universe belongs to one, so it does equally to the total of all upon whom the joint inheritances are bestowed.[33]

## Is There A Place For Me?

Yes, it is His work and His glory to bring to pass your immortality and eternal life![34] He has prepared a mansion for you. "If it were not so," He said, "I would have told you."

> *. . . I go to prepare a place for you.*
>
> *And if I go and prepare a place for you, I will*
> *come again, and receive you unto myself; that where I*
> *am, there ye may be also.*
>
> *And whither I go ye know, and the way ye know.*[35]

We need not walk alone, neither should our hearts be afraid. His eyes

---

[30] See Romans 8:13-14, 16.

[31] Romans 8:17.

[32] *Teachings of the Prophet Joseph Smith*, p. 347.

[33] *Mormon Doctrine*, see "Joint Heirs with Jesus Christ," pp. 361-62 (1st Edition).

[34] See Moses 1:39.

[35] John 14:2-4.

are upon us. He is in our midst. Yet we cannot see him. The Lord said:

> *But the day soon cometh that ye shall see me, and*
> *know that I am . . .*
>
> *Wherefore, gird up your loins and be prepared.*
> *Behold, the kingdom is yours, and the enemy shall not*
> *overcome.*[36]

Herein lies the power and the way where by you can pass by the gods
and the angels to have glory sealed upon your head "and a continuation of
the seeds forever and ever."[37] "Verily, thus saith the Lord: It shall come to
pass that every soul who:

1.  Forsaketh his sins and

2.  cometh unto me,

3.  and calleth on my name,

4.  and obeyeth my voice,

5.  and keepeth my commandments, shall see my face and
    know that I am.[38]

## When Am I Converted?

As used in the scriptures "converted" implies not merely mental
acceptance of Jesus and His teachings, but also a motivating faith in Him
and in His Gospel—a faith that works a transformation. While conversion
may be accomplished in stages, one is not really converted in the full sense
of the term unless and until he is at heart a new person. "Born again" is the
scriptural term. Paul taught the Romans that such an one would walk in
newness of life, a new creature, the old man is no more.

Peter taught that by walking in this "newness of life" one escapes the
corruption that is in the world. He becomes a partaker "of the divine

---

[36] D&C 38:7-9.
[37] D&C 132:19.
[38] D&C 93:1.

nature." One who walks in newness of life is converted.

From some of the Savior's sayings it would seem that there might even be people in high places whose conversion is not complete. . . .

Membership in the Church and conversion are not necessarily synonymous. Being converted and having a testimony are not necessarily the same thing either.

A testimony comes when the Holy Ghost gives the earnest seeker a witness of the truth. A moving testimony vitalizes faith: that is, it induces repentance and obedience to the commandments. Conversion, on the other hand, is the fruit of, or the reward for repentance and obedience. (Of course, one's testimony continues to increase as he is converted.)

Conversion is effected by divine forgiveness, which remits sins. The sequence is something like this. An honest seeker hears the message. He asked the Lord in prayer if it is true. The Holy Spirit gives him a witness. This is testimony. If one's testimony is strong enough, he repents and obeys the commandments. By such obedience he receives divine forgiveness which remits sin. Thus he is converted to a newness of life. His spirit is healed.[39]

## A Personal Encouragement

From several sources come encouragement for us to keep trying and striving to achieve the great privilege of once again being in the presence of the Savior and our Heavenly Father.

SUCCESS

You can't fell trees without some chips.
You can't achieve without some slips.
Unless you try, you'll wonder why
Good fortune seems to pass you by.
Success is not for those who quail;
She gives her best to those who fail.

---

[39] See Marion G. Romney, Conference Report, October 1963, pp. 23-24.

And then, with courage twice as great,
Takes issue once again with fate.
'Tis better far to risk a fall,
Than not to make attempt at all.

—Anonymous

## GOOD TIMBER

The tree that never had to fight
For sun and sky and air and light,
But stood out in the open plain
And always got its share of rain,
Never became a forest king
But lived and died a scrubby thing.

The man who never had to toil
[By hand or mind mid life's turmoil]
Who never had to win his share
Of sun and sky and light and air,
Never became a manly man
But lived and died as he began.

Good timber does not grow with ease,
The stronger wind, the [tougher] trees.
The further sky, the greater length,
The more the storm, the more the strength.
By sun and cold, by rain and snow,
In trees or men good timbers grow.

Where thickest [stands] the forest growth
We find the patriarchs of both.
And they hold converse with the stars
Whose broken branches show the scars
Of many winds and much of strife—
This is the common law of life.

—Douglas Malloch[40]

---

[40] *Best-Loved Poems of the LDS People* [Deseret Book, 1996], 248-249, with modifications
from original version as shown in brackets ([]).

DON'T QUIT

When things go wrong, as they sometimes will,
When the road you're trodding seems all uphill,
When the funds are low and the debts are high,
And you want to smile, but you have to sigh,
When care is pressing you down a bit,
Rest, If you must—but don't you quit.

Life is queer, with its twists and turns,
As everyone of us sometimes learns,
And many a failure turns about
When he might have won if he stuck it out;
[Stick to your task], though the pace seems slow,
You may succeed with another blow.

Often the goal is nearer than
It seems to a faint and faltering man.
Often the struggler has given up
When he might have captured the victor's cup
And he learned too late, when the night slipped down,
How close he was to the golden crown.

Success is a failure turned inside out—
The silver tints of the clouds of doubt—
And you never can tell how close you are,
It may be near when it seems afar;
So stick to the fight when you're hardest hit—
It's when things seem worst that you mustn't quit.

                                        —Anonymous[41]

A firm commitment to the principles of the Gospel is important in developing faith. Perhaps the experience of a young man playing basketball in Madison Square Garden with unconquerable determination may serve as a good example of commitment to all of us.

A particular university basketball team was playing in the semi-final

---

[41] *Best-Loved Poems of the LDS People* [Deseret Book, 1996], 307-308, with modification from original version as shown in brackets ([]).

game of the National Invitational Tournament in Madison Square Garden. The team was behind six points with 30 seconds remaining. In the days before the three-point rule, there was little hope for this basketball team to make up six points. One young player had such a driving determination, he stole the ball and with one hand shot it from the middle of the floor, the ball went through the basket touching only the net. What a beautiful sound when the basketball touches just the net—a clean two-point shot!

To the amazement of the thousands of people in Madison Square Garden with only 15 seconds left, this young man repeated this same feat, again the ball "swished" through the basket from the middle of the court. One would have thought this 5'10" young man didn't have strength enough to throw the ball that far even once. Then as the gun was fired, he grabbed the ball in the end of the court opposite his basket and with three opposing players smothering him, he heaved the ball full court to tie the score. The audience was electrified. No need to tell you that in the overtime this young man and his team won easily. The crowd stormed to the floor, and the small basketball player was bounced around in the outstretched hands of the wild and enthusiastic fans. This was the longest basketball goal ever made in Madison Square Garden. Courage and commitment of this quality cannot be defeated.

You must believe that the Kingdom of Heaven is incomplete without you. Though you may not now know it, you are being watched over very carefully. There is great joy in your every step forward. So long as there is one more breath we may draw, our eternal score can be improved. God bless you with a will to win and an unyielding desire become His son or His daughter.

## Thoughts For Meditation

1. If we call upon God with all the energy of our hearts, Satan may be bound and have no more place in us.

2. The gift of charity grows within me as I lose disposition to criticize others.

3. Those who love the Lord and keep his commandments have as their objective the cleansing, purifying, and sanctifying

of their souls.

4.   Those who are continually led by the Spirit of God, which is to say by the voice of His counsels, are the sons and daughters of God.

5.   We should not feel that we walk alone; for His eyes are upon us and He is in our midst.

6.   You must believe that the Kingdom of Heaven is incomplete without *you*.

# CHAPTER EIGHT

# Blessings of the Patriarchal Priesthood

Celestial society is patriarchal in its organization. The divine patriarchal order existed in eternity before the creation of the earth; and the law that pertains to the celestial family was established upon this earth in the early ages of the world. It came down from the fathers, from the beginning of time, yea, even from the beginning, or before the foundations of the earth. This family order is based upon the principles and ordinances of the Gospel by which the obedient become sons and daughters of Jesus Christ in the divine endowments that lead to eternal life.

Next to Christ, Adam presides as a father in eternal life over the righteous of the earth. Under him, each righteous man has a similar right to preside over his worthy posterity in the flesh, including those who are adopted into his family through the covenants and sealing powers of the priesthood. Having become members of the family of Christ by obeying the Gospel, the faithful must go to the House of the Lord and receive the covenants of the priesthood by which they are organized according to the law of the divine patriarchal order. Each generation of this divine system must be sealed from Adam until the latest age of time.

The patriarchal order was perpetuated through the ancient patriarchs. Among the Israelites as a chosen people, the Lord also sought to establish the divine family system. Accordingly, certain branches of Israel were given promises of power and authority within the over-all system. To Ephraim was given the right to preside over the Patriarchal Priesthood. The sons of Aaron were given the right to preside over the Aaronic Priesthood. And the sons of David were given the promise of royal, or political, power in Israel.

As a part of the restoration of all things in the latter days, the patriarchal order is to be reestablished upon the earth before the Lord comes in His glory. To this end the Gospel must be preached and the branches of Israel gathered and given their promised rights within the divine system. Zion must be built up according to the ancient pattern. Christ's kingdom will be established, that when He comes He may reign over the earth by means of the divine patriarchal order, as King of Kings and Lord of Lords.

The Celestial kingdom consists of a divine family order that is patriarchal in its organization. According to Joseph Smith, this celestial order is "a kingdom of priests and kings to God, and the Lamb, forever." By complying with the covenants and ordinances of the Holy Priesthood as now administered in the Temples of God, wives are sealed to righteous husbands and children to righteous parents in a divine family order. In this way, one generation is sealed to another back in time to the great patriarchs. Ultimately all the righteous are organized in this way under Jesus Christ. This is the celestial family of Christ, over which he presides as God and Father.

A man who lacks the faith to be born into this "newness of life" which the Gospel makes possible, and who thereafter fails to mature in the endowments of the Holy Spirit, so that he can develop the same divine truths and powers that lead to eternal life with his wife and children in the flesh, cannot be made a father over his posterity in the resurrection. It should be stressed that birth in the flesh as an heir to certain blessings does not guarantee that an individual will receive that to which he has a claim by promise.

Only by receiving the new and everlasting covenant of marriage could Abraham receive the promise that his posterity would continue to multiply out of the world; the promise where faithful fathers are to be priests and kings (and women are to be priestesses and queens) over their ever-increasing posterity through all subsequent generations of time, and throughout all eternity, worlds without end.

These keys descended upon Joseph. Thereafter the right to preside over the patriarchal priesthood was centered by promise in the lineage of his son Ephraim. Joseph Smith was told that he obtained rights to this order by and through the loins of Joseph. In this way, the patriarchal priesthood was restored and the keys of presidency assigned to the proper lineage in the flesh. It now remains for the saints to develop a true family-centered society.[1]

The purpose of the organizations within the church is the perfecting of the Saints until they come to a unity of the faith and of the knowledge of the Son of God, unto a perfect man, unto the measure of the stature of the fullness of Christ.[2] Only the laws, ordinances, and organizations which relate to the highest of exaltations are revealed in our scriptures and by present-day revelation. These all relate to the perfecting of the earthly family unit within the context of the patriarchal order. Detailed requirements and bounds relating to all other kingdoms have not been revealed to mankind. It is our responsibility to embrace the fullness of the Gospel and lay a firm foundation in our early years so that when the time comes to receive the blessings in the temple there will be nothing which stands between us and our going there worthily.

## The Foundation Years

Preparation to go to the House of the Lord and receive the sealing ordinances should begin as soon as we understand and embrace the Gospel. Too many learn too late that even though a kind Heavenly Father may forgive us for time lost, it is lost just the same. Some years ago an article appeared in the *Improvement Era* which presented this thought clearly.

---

[1] See Hyrum L. Andrus, *Doctrinal Commentary on the Pearl of Great Price,* Deseret Book, Chapter 11.

[2] Ephesians 4:13.

Many marry when they're supposed to be experiencing the joys of youth and then seek the joys of youth when they're supposed to be married . . . they learn to cook after they're married and study the scriptures after they arrive in the mission field . . . or they learn to behave properly after they've been embarrassed . . . or value gospel principles after they suffered the pangs of repentance . . . or they affect the look of "big ladies" when that special freshness of youth is still upon them . . . or they think about being gentlemanly after they've asked for a date . . . or go through the motions of "being in love" when they should be learning about friendship.

Too much too soon, or too little too late can take the bloom off achievement, personal growth, real love. With only one chance at life, we'd better check our timing. For though some say, "better late than never," it is infinitely better to do what needs to be done when it should be done.[3] Someone has said that the selection of a companion is of such a consequence that, if made on the basis of unsound reason and emotion, the efforts of a lifetime may not undo the effects.

Preparations for the great event of your marriage have included many eons of time. Yet in the matter of a few hours in the Temple of the Lord one closes the long period of being separate and alone—never to be alone agin. If both partners are faithful to their covenants, they will subsequently have glory and honor added upon their heads forever and ever.

Going to the temple for eternal marriage is one of the greatest achievements and purposes in this mortal existence. The House of the Lord is the home of the Lord. The temple is a place for instruction and a place for covenants. Many blessings and revelations occur in this Holy house. This is where the Lord will come when he returns to the earth. The temple is where ceremonies pertaining to godliness are presented.

## The Priesthood Endowment

Before a person can be married (sealed as husband and wife) in the temple, he or she must receive the ordinances of the endowment. What comprises the temple endowment? The Prophet Brigham Young gave this

---

[3] See Ecclesiastes 3:1-8.

excellent definition.

> *Your endowment is, to receive all those ordinances in the House of the Lord, which are necessary for you, after you have departed this life, to enable you to walk back into the presence of your Father, passing the angels who stand as sentinels, being enabled to give them the key words, the signs and tokens pertaining to the Holy Priesthood, and gain your eternal exaltation in spite of earth and hell.[4]*

As one receives his endowments, he will be given instructions pertaining to the creating and peopling of the earth. Each person will be given insight as to what is involved in being exalted. These are sacred matters and are to be given only to those worthy to go into the temple. Elder Talmage has given us a clear description of the endowment:

> *The temple endowment, as administered in modern temples, comprises instruction relating to the significance and sequence of past dispensations, and the importance of the present as the greatest and grandest era in human history. This course of instruction includes a recital of the most prominent events of the creative periods, the condition of our first parents in the Garden of Eden, their disobedience and consequent expulsion from that blissful abode, their condition in the lone and dreary world when doomed to live by labor and sweat, the plan of redemption by which the great transgression may be atoned, the period of the great apostasy, the restoration of the Gospel with all its ancient powers and privileges, the absolute and indispensable condition of personal purity and devotion to the right in present life, and a strict compliance with Gospel requirements. . . .*
>
> *The ordinances of the endowment embody certain obligations on the part of the individual, such as*

---

[4] *Discourses of Brigham Young*, sel. John A. Widtsoe [1941], 416.

*covenant and promise to observe the law of strict virtue and chastity, to be charitable, benevolent, tolerant and pure; to devote both talent and material means to the spread of truth and the uplifting of the race; to maintain devotion to the cause of truth; and to seek in every way to contribute to the great preparation that the earth may be made ready to receive her King,—the Lord Jesus Christ. With the taking of each covenant and the assuming of each obligation a promised blessing is pronounced, contingent upon the faithful observance of the conditions.*

*No jot, iota, or tittle of the temple rites is otherwise than uplifting and sanctifying. In every detail the endowment ceremony contributes to covenants of morality of life, consecration of person to high ideals, devotion to truth, patriotism to nation, and allegiance to God . . .[5]*

The endowment ordinances enrich the lives of the Latter-day Saints in many ways. Elder McConkie states that:

*The one receiving the ordinance is given power from God. Recipients are endowed with power from on High. A recipient is also endowed with information and knowledge. They receive an education relative to the Lord's purposes and plans . . .[6]*

When sealed at the altar for time and eternity the Latter-day Saint can be the recipient of glorious blessings, powers and honors. There is nothing in this life that can be a greater blessing or nothing in this life that would have greater assistance to godliness in the worlds to come than for a member of the Church to receive his endowment and then be sealed to his companion forever.

---

[5] James E. Talmage, *The House of the Lord,* Bookcraft, pp. 99-101.
[6] Bruce R. McConkie, *Mormon Doctrine,* Endowments, p. 209 (1st Edition).

## Sacredness of Temple Marriage

Temple marriage is not the new and everlasting covenant but it is an everlasting covenant embraced in the new and everlasting covenant which encompasses all ordinances. Exaltation cannot be received without the endowment and sealing. A church member who has received these sacred ordinances will not only be prepared for future progression in the worlds to come, but will also be able to participate in the great work to be done during the millennium.

The veil that separates the living from the dead will be withdrawn at that time, and mortal men and ancients will converse. Latter-day Saints will need to be worthy, knowledgeable, committed, and in a position to carry on the work of the Lord when He comes. This work will be done through the organization of His Church and the power of the priesthood.

When a couple is united for time and eternity in the House of the Lord, they will be asked, by the Lord's servant, to become one. There is true joy in oneness. This means each companion must be true, loyal, and devoted to the other. There cannot be cheating in any way, because when one of the partners cheats they become two and sorrow will result. If cheating does occur, whether it be financially, spiritually, morally, or in any other way, there should be immediate repentance and oneness achieved as soon as possible.

It is not good for man to be alone; and therefore hath it been ordained that "a man leave his father and his mother and shall cleave unto his wife; and they shall be one flesh."[7] for, "neither is the man without the woman, neither the woman without the man, in the Lord."[8] Joseph F. Smith stated that, "The lawful association of the sexes is ordained of God, not only as the sole means of race perpetuation, but for the development of the higher faculties and nobler traits of human nature, which the love-inspired companionship of man and woman alone can insure . . . and, if participated in with right intent is honorable and sanctifying."[9]

---

[7] Genesis 2:18, 24.
[8] 1 Corinthians 11:11.
[9] President Joseph F. Smith, *The Improvement Era,* Vol. 20, p. 739.

Obtaining a temple recommend signifies that you have met the requirements to enter the House of the Lord—there to receive the final pronouncement of blessings relating to this part of our eternal existence. There you receive a partner with whom to share life's experiences—one with whom you feel a mutual uplift and from whom you derive comfort and encouragement. Your marriage then marks the end of the foundation period and the beginning of everything that is of an exalting and everlasting nature. Remember this, after several decades together you will just begin to know what love really is.

There is no problem that a Latter-day Saint couple cannot solve if they both are humble. There is no room for pride or vanity. Confide in your companion when you are tempted, struggling, or when you are weighed down; for the Lord will bless you in resolving your weaknesses as you go to him with a humble spirit and fasting. It is important that both always show the many courtesies which indicate love for each other.

The House of the Lord is the best place for the man and the woman to be together. There is nothing more beautiful than the joy received in the temple when a husband and wife go through an endowment session and meet each other on the other side of the veil in the Celestial Room. Both realize at that time that each is working toward being worthy of the other, keeping the commandments the Lord has so explicitly given, and demonstrating that there is nothing more important in life than being together. When this sanctified relationship is sealed by the Holy Spirit of Promise these two become eternally one and are evermore His sons and His daughters. These are the highest blessings of which the Lord has made reference. They may be ours through a proper understanding of the doctrines of the kingdom, commitment and effort.

## Thoughts For Meditation

1.  The organization and administration of the Celestial Kingdom will be through a family order.

2.  Each of us must be worthy to receive the sealing blessings of the temple and thereafter be true and faithful to the covenants associated with that ordinance.

3.  During my life time I must find the proper "time and season" to accomplish each of the significant requirements for mortality.

4.  The selection of the right eternal companion is the most significant and far-reaching decision I will make in mortality.

5.  The Patriarchal Order of the priesthood will allow me to become a king or queen and a priest or priestess forever.

CHAPTER NINE

# After Thou Art Converted

Aconvert is one who has put off the natural man and become a saint through the atonement of the Lord Jesus Christ.

> . . . *and becometh as a child, submissive, meek, humble, patient, full of love, willing to submit to all things which the Lord seeth fit to inflict upon him, even as a child doth submit to his father.*[1]

True conversion affects every aspect of life. In a very literal sense the person becomes a new creature,[2] and receives the image of the Lord in his countenance.[3] This new creature is a work of the Holy Ghost.

It is not enough to have a testimony of the gospel. Each must press forward until fully converted. In 1837, the Prophet was admonished to say to the twelve that if they would be faithful, the Lord would convert them, and heal them.[4] This may seem peculiar since all had entered into the apostleship with testimonies of the gospel and had served some two years

---

[1] Mosiah 3:19.
[2] See Mosiah 27:26. See also Romans 8.
[3] See Alma 5:14.
[4] See D&C 112:13.

in their callings. To become converted is to be valiant in the testimony of Jesus. Speaking of many Latter-day Saints, the Lord, in the revelation known as *The Vision*, declared:

> *These are they who are not valiant in the testimony of Jesus; wherefore, they obtain not the crown over the kingdom of our God.*[5]

It must be remembered that one cannot begin to be valiant in the testimony of Jesus until he is baptized by one having authority. The Lord showed the prophet that many members of the Church would be assigned to the terrestrial kingdom because they failed to see the relationship between "just attending" and being valiant.[6]

## Signs that Follow True Believers

In every gospel dispensation the Lord has promised great blessings to the true believers.

> *. . . signs shall follow them that believe—in my name shall they cast out devils; they shall speak with new tongues; they shall take up serpents; and if they drink any deadly thing it shall not hurt them; they shall lay hands on the sick and they shall recover;*
>
> *And whosoever shall believe in my name, doubting nothing, unto him will I confirm all my words, even unto the ends of the earth.*[7]

Notice though that these gifts which produce signs are a by-product of believing and faithful service, and in fact are produced by faith. The effect is to strengthen those who are already spiritually inclined. Their chief purpose is not to convert people to the truth, but to reward and bless those already converted.

We are told in the scriptures that these things are reserved for the

---

[5] D&C 76:79.
[6] See Revelations 3:16.
[7] Mormon 9:24-25.

faithful, for there shall be no witness until after the trial of your faith.

> *Yea, signs come by faith, unto mighty works, for without faith no man pleaseth God; and with whom God is angry he is not well pleased; wherefore, unto such he showeth no signs, only in wrath to their condemnation.*[8]

Signs are sacred grants of divine favor reserved for the faithful and concerning which the recipients are commanded not to boast.

> *. . . a commandment I give unto them, that they shall not boast themselves of these things, neither speak them before the world; for these things are given unto you for your profit and for salvation.*[9]

> *Remember that that which cometh from above is sacred, and must be spoken with care, and by constraint of the Spirit; and in this there is no condemnation, and ye receive the Spirit through prayer; wherefore, without this there remaineth condemnation.*[10]

## Characteristics of a Zion People

As important as what occurs inside the follower of Christ is the outward change. His sons and daughters have a different feeling toward their brothers and sisters.

It would be a thrill to have a full account of the development of the City of Enoch and more than just a two page historical account concerning the people of Nephi after the resurrected Lord visited them. Surely we could learn much about the dealings of a just people one with another. Nevertheless, these few glimpses into their lives should cause this people (the Latter-day Saints) to ponder present conditions and consider how we might be like them.

---

[8] D&C 63:11.
[9] D&C 84:73.
[10] D&C 63:64.

*. . . there were no contentions and disputations among them, and every man did deal justly one with another.*

*And they had all things common among them; therefore there were not rich and poor, bond and free, but they were all made free, and partakers of the heavenly gift.*

*And there were great and marvelous works wrought by the disciples of Jesus, insomuch that they did heal the sick, and raise the dead, and cause the lame to walk, and the blind to receive their sight, and the deaf to hear; and all manner of miracles did they work among the children of men; and in nothing did they work miracles save it were in the name of Jesus.*

*And the Lord did prosper them exceedingly in the land . . . and, it came to pass that the people . . . did wax strong, and did multiply exceedingly fast, and became an exceedingly fair and delightsome people.*

*And they were married, and given in marriage, and were blessed according to the . . . promises which the Lord had made unto them.*

*And they did not walk any more after the performances and ordinances of the law of Moses; but they did walk after the commandments which they had received from their Lord and their God, continuing in fasting and prayer, and in meeting together oft both to pray and to hear the word of the Lord.*

*And it came to pass that there was no contention in the land, because of the love of God which did dwell in the hearts of the people.*

*And there were no envyings, nor strifes, nor tumults, nor whoredomes, nor lyings, nor murders, nor any manner of lasciviousness . . . neither were they Lamanites, nor any manner of ites; but they were in one, the children of Christ, and heirs to the kingdom of*

*God.*

*And how blessed were they! For the Lord did bless them in all their doings . . . and surely there could not be a happier people among all the people who had been created by the hand of God.*[11]

Commanding us in our own dispensation, the Lord declared to the Prophet that the Saints of the Latter-day can, by hearkening unto the counsels of the Lord, become pure and therefore bring forth "blessings upon her (Zion) and upon her generations forever and ever."[12]

*. . . Behold, if Zion do these things she shall prosper, . . .*

*And the nations of the earth shall honor her, and shall say: Surely Zion . . . cannot fall, neither be moved out of her place, for God is there, and the hand of the Lord is there;*

*Therefore, verily, thus saith the Lord, let Zion rejoice, for this is Zion—THE PURE IN HEART; therefore, let Zion rejoice, while all the wicked shall mourn.*

*For behold, and lo, vengeance cometh speedily upon the ungodly as the whirlwind; and who shall escape it?*

*The Lord's scourge shall pass over by night and by day, and the report thereof shall vex all people; yea, it shall not be stayed until the Lord come;*

*For the indignation of the Lord is kindled against their abominations and all their wicked works.*

*Nevertheless, Zion shall escape if she observe to do all things whatsoever I have commanded her.*[13]

---

[11] 4 Nephi 2, 3, 5, 7, 10, 11-12, 15-18, 16.
[12] D&C 97:28.
[13] D&C 97:18, 19, 21-25.

A New Way of Life

Some personal characteristics and attitudes of those who cleanse their souls and live by these principles might be useful in measuring our own progress toward total conversion. These are characteristics which each of us can acquire and make a part of our lives.

1. They have ceased murmuring when called upon to give of their time in the Church.

2. They contribute a full tithe, that the building up of the kingdom of God might roll forth.

3. They donate a generous fast offering in response to the critical need to feed the poor and clothe the naked. I know a man who increases his monthly gift each time he receives a raise. Do they really care about His little ones?

4. After having tasted of the fruit of the tree, they desire that others might partake also. Opportunity is taken to share the gospel with others. Converts from within or without the Church are seen as equally exciting to them.

5. They listen carefully for every word of counsel from their Home Teachers, Priesthood leaders, Bishop, Stake Presidency, General Authorities, and the Prophet—then incorporate these things into their daily living.

6. They know that families can be bound together in love and singleness of purpose through regular home evenings, supplemented by regular scripture reading where the Father, as patriarch, teaches the words of the Lord and reveals His will to each member of the family.

7. They have found that there is a constant need to call upon Father in mighty prayer—giving thanks and seeking divine inspiration concerning a full understanding of this probationary state. When this knowledge comes they find the Heavens a never ending source of light and knowledge.

8. They understand that every position in the Church is equally important and that the creation of another "City of Enoch" can come only with each learning and doing his duty. After all, if all men everywhere were walking up to all the light and knowledge available to man and were all perfect, still only twelve would be in the Quorum of the Twelve Apostles and one would be the Prophet.

9. They understand that all blessings after this life can be claimed only by being sealed to righteous forefathers through the ordinances performed in the Temples of the Lord. And that after performing the work for all direct descendants, they must branch out to extend the blessings to all their ancestors.

10. Their teachings are filled with faith and power. They speak with authority, having the Holy Ghost as their constant companion.

11. They participate freely in the fullness of the Gospel, and attend to all their duties being filled with the Spirit so that it might radiate to others.

12. With hope in Christ they look forward, somewhat longingly, to the day of their redemption and rest in the Lord. Life is sweet, because they know what awaits them just beyond the veil.

## Feed My Sheep

But while left in the flesh, the converted soul does not waste away his days dreaming about mansions on high. Nor does he ever find a lack of mountains to climb. The Lord's injunction to Peter, "Feed my sheep" heralds an invitation to become involved.

John Whitmer wished for this involvement and to know that which would be of greatest worth to him. The Lord responded:

> *And now, behold, I say unto you, that the thing*
> *which will be of the most worth unto you will be to*
> *declare repentance unto this people, that you may*
> *bring souls unto me, that you may rest with them in the*
> *kingdom of my Father.[14]*

An even more personal and specific invitation was given to Peter after the Last Supper. The Lord took him aside and said,

> *Simon, Simon, behold, Satan hath desired to have*
> *you, that he may sift you as wheat:*
>
> *But I have prayed for thee, that thy faith fail not:*
> *and when thou art converted, strengthen thy brethren.[15]*

And so, when *thou* are converted, thy days may be used up in strengthening the hearts of the inhabitants of Zion and in bringing souls out of darkness into the light.[16]

The Good Shepherd suggested that without this true conversion we are likely to behave as an hireling; who, when the wolf cometh, leaveth the sheep and fleeth. He careth not for the sheep. Certainly he would not lay down his life for them.[17]

Following are examples where those having responsibility for the sheep were truly converted and exhibited great concern for those they were entrusted to teach. The first comes from the lives of the Sons of Mosiah, who desired to impart the word of God to their brethren, the Lamanites.

> *Now they were desirous that salvation should be*
> *declared to every creature, for they could not bear that*
> *any human soul should perish; yea, even the very*
> *thoughts that any should endure endless torment did*
> *cause them to quake and tremble.[18]*

The second example comes from the life of Alma the younger, who

---

[14] D&C 15:6
[15] Luke 22:31-32.
[16] See Alma 26:21-22.
[17] See John 10:11-15.
[18] Mosiah 28:3.

after he was converted, sought also to touch the lives of others. He headed a mission to reclaim the apostate Zoramites. The record contains his pleadings unto the Lord in their behalf.

> *O Lord, my heart is exceedingly sorrowful; wilt thou comfort my soul in Christ. O Lord, wilt thou grant unto me that I may have strength, that I may suffer with patience these afflictions which shall come upon me, because of the iniquity of this people.*
>
> *O Lord, wilt thou grant unto us that we may have success in bringing them again unto thee in Christ.*
>
> *Behold, O Lord, their souls are precious, and many of them are our brethren; therefore, give unto us, O Lord, power and wisdom that we may bring these, our brethren, again unto thee.*[19]

They cared! And so did Nephi when in his parting testimony he expressed great concern for his people.

> *. . . For I pray continually for them by day, and mine eyes water my pillow by night, because of them; and I cry unto my God in faith, and I know that he will hear my cry.*[20]

Many saints have experienced a similar thrill in strengthening their brethren in our day. For example, there was a young man in a ward who was a priest and wanted as little activity as possible. In fact, he generally slept through priesthood meetings. During the week, his Bishop made it a point to get better acquainted with him, to learn of his likes and dislikes, to know his weaknesses and his strengths. The Bishop found that one of this young man's great strengths was playing basketball. So during the week, they arranged to have some basketball games in the gymnasium, one-on-one, having some good wholesome fun. As time went on they became much closer. One Sunday morning when Priesthood Meeting was over the bishop went to the priest's apartment and knocked on the door. There was

---

[19] Alma 31:31, 34-35.
[20] 2 Nephi 33:3.

not a sound, because he was asleep. On the second knock there was a groan and on the third knock the young man wanted to know who it was. He was embarrassed, but invited the bishop in. As they sat at his bedside and discussed a few matters of the day, the bishop asked for a favor. The young man wanted to know what it was because he would do most anything the bishop would ask. The bishop told him he wanted him to attend the fast and testimony meeting and bear his testimony that morning. This was a tough assignment, but he responded and bore a sweet testimony. This inactive priest became more and more active and shortly thereafter was called to serve as a full-time missionary for the Church.

From my own experience I remember my first assignment in a bishopric was to activate a good community person who had been completely inactive in the church. He would not allow the home teachers to visit him and the bishop told me that this inactive brother would be my responsibility. I told the bishop I would have him visited before the month was over. He lived in an upstairs apartment and drove a yellow pickup truck. Many times I passed by his apartment trying to locate him, and either there was no light in his apartment or his truck would be gone. As it neared the end of the month, I knew that I must visit him, so I decided to try once again late in the evening. But there was still no light on in his home. So I was prompted to return early the next morning at 4:00 a.m. I knew that he had to arise sooner or later and prepare for work. So I waited in front of his home and when the light in his apartment went on I immediately went upstairs and knocked on the door and introduced myself to him, telling him I was his home teacher. This man appeared to be completely appalled. He said, "Any person who is willing to come here at this time of the day to see me is welcome. Come in." Needless to say, in a period of time we had this good brother active in the Church.

There are many of our brethren and sisters in the gospel who cry out for help, but are not heard. Strengthening the members in our area is one of the most joyous experiences in this life.

### Again, What About Me?

Dag Hammerskjold once said, "It is more noble to give yourself completely to one individual than to labor diligently for the salvation of the masses. Remember the worth of souls is great in the sight of God."

> *And if it so be that you should labor all your days in crying repentance unto this people, and bring, save it be one soul unto me, how great shall be your joy with him in the kingdom of my father![21]*

> *Wherefore, (saith the Lord), I call upon the weak things of the world, those who are unlearned and despised, to thrash the nations by the power of my Spirit;*

> *And their (your) arm shall be my arm . . . and they (you) shall fight manfully for me.[22]*

Being thus compelled and led by the Spirit, treasures can be laid up for yourself in heaven. These treasures are made up of precious souls, your brothers and sisters. Surely, the Lord will provide, for you shall be given in the very hour that which you should speak unto them.[23] And you shall "suffer no manner of afflictions, save it were swallowed up in the joy of Christ."[24]

> *Brethren, if any of you do err from the truth, and one convert him;*

> *Let him know, that he which converteth the sinner from the error of his way shall save a soul from death, and shall hide a multitude of sins.[25]*

> *For behold the field is white already to harvest; and lo, he that thrusteth in his sickle with his might, the same layeth up in store that he perisheth not, but bringeth salvation to his soul.[26]*

After one is converted, and knows wherein he speaks, he should

---

[21] D&C 18:10, 15.
[22] D& C 35:13-14.
[23] See D&C 84:85 and 100:6.
[24] Alma 31:38.
[25] James 5:19-20.
[26] D&C 4:4.

strengthen his brethren. You can find the lost sheep and feed His young lambs. You can have joy with them everlastingly in the kingdom of our Father.

## Thoughts For Meditation

1.  When one is converted, he literally becomes a new person and receives the image of the Lord in his countenance.

2.  The chief purpose of spiritual signs is not to convert people to the truth, but rather to reward and bless those already converted.

3.  What personal characteristics and attitudes do I have that would indicate progress toward total conversion?

4.  Latter-day Saints can also help establish a Zion people just as did Enoch and the people of Nephi at the time of the Lord's appearance among them.

5.  Strengthening our brothers and sisters in the Gospel of Jesus Christ is one of the most joyous experiences in life.

# CHAPTER TEN

# Quiet Consistency

T erms which are associated with overcoming the world include: being born again, being sanctified by the Spirit, being sealed by the Holy Spirit of Promise, receiving the Second Comforter, and having one's calling and election made sure. These describe achievements of those who will be redeemed.

> . . . *These are they which follow the Lamb withersoever he goeth. These were (are) redeemed from among men, being the first fruits unto God and to the Lamb.*
>
> *And in their mouth was (is) found no guile: for they are without fault before the throne of God.*[1]

These weary not in righteous doing. "Doing good is a pleasure a joy beyond measure; a blessing of duty and love." A sweet peace fills their souls and heaven is within their breast.

These are the enlightened years. Which years, regardless of number, begin their reckoning when a soul lays hold upon the peace and calmness promised by the Savior and he knows that his name is written in the

---

[1] Revelations 14:4-5.

Lamb's Book of Life.

These are the quiet years. Not that all about has ceased its commotion; rather like one who on a lonesome road hath walked in fear and dread, but having once turned round, walks on and turns no more his head.[2] Though earth and hell combine to hedge up the way, he presses forward—with his eyes firmly fixed upon the goal. Of such it may be said, "The best of life will always be further on."[3] Endless are his works and endless his enjoyments. "Surely goodness and mercy shall follow [him] all the days of [his] life: and [he] shall dwell in the house of the Lord forever."[4]

## Strength for the Day

Father has not placed us here for some four-score years to reap only sorrow and misery. Though these things as we have seen, were in a measure meant to be; our understanding of mortal life is often too incomplete, too limited to give clear vision. Though we do not see what lies dimly at a distance, we must resolve to do what clearly lies at hand.

Thoreau urged his reader, "Don't waste the years struggling for things that are unimportant. Don't burden yourself with possessions. Keep your needs and wants simple, and enjoy what you have." "Happiness is not so much in having what you want, as it is in wanting what you have," said a wise rabbi.

The Lord in His infinite wisdom will provide all that you can wisely use. If this turns out to be less than what you had hoped for, be patient, and consistent; by and by you will "inherit thrones, kingdoms, principalities, and powers, dominions, all heights and depths . . . and a continuation of the seeds forever and ever."[5]

Be willing to bear whatever burden is placed upon you. Do one thing at a time. There are sufficient days and years allotted to accomplish all you were foreordained to do. Confusion comes when we try to do too many

---

[2] See Samuel Taylor Coleridge, *The Ancient Mariner.*
[3] Sir William Mulock.
[4] Psalms 23:6.
[5] D&C 132:19.

things at once. Allow each task its appointed time. Sir William Olsen is quoted as teaching a group of ambitious young people that, "the load of tomorrow, added to that of yesterday, carried today makes the strongest falter." No one is expected to run faster than he has strength. When burdens seem too numerous to bear—compare your life to an hourglass—note how only one grain of sand can slip through at a time.[6] They cannot be hurried nor can the pace be slackened.

Robert Louis Stevenson put it this way, "anyone can carry his burden, however hard until nightfall. Anyone can do his work, however hard, for one day. Anyone can live sweetly, patiently, lovingly, purely, til the sun goes down." At dusk, calmly close forever the door behind you. Open the next with the rising sun—one at a time. So often we are prone to wish away precious time saying, "If only I can get through this week" or "Next month I'll not be so busy." Whatever life exacts, little or much, learn to profit from and enjoy each hour of every day. Fill up your days with new understandings, new enjoyments, and new expectations. Should choices of how to use one's time become perplexing, simply ask, "A hundred million years from now, will it still matter?" Some things will and others will not. In finishing the course successfully, clear perspective, vision, and quiet consistency counts.

## This, Too, Shall Pass Away

From all these experiences comes a courage to face the future fearlessly, knowing that each step forward takes us closer to "home." However hard our burdens are to bear, we will be able to remain firm in the faith if we know that it shall pass away.

Even the heavens and the earth shall pass away, but His promises will not; for they shall all be fulfilled and be answered upon the heads of the faithful. The outpouring of light and knowledge brings with it a quiet longing—a homesickness for our "real home." This vision brings joy to the twilight years. When the mortal tabernacle finally slows down, there is time for reflections, meditation, and a summing up.

---

[6] James Gordon Gilkey.

So long thy pow'r hath blest me, sure it still
Will lead me on
O'er moor and fen, o'er crag and torrent, till
The night is gone.
And with the morn those angel faces smile
Which I have loved long since, and lost a-while![7]

SUN AND MOUNTAIN MEET

"Look," I say
"Sunset."
But I forget
That far away
An islander
Wipes Morning
From his eyes
And watches
The same sun
Rise.
What's birth?
And death?
What's near
Or far?
It all depends
On where you are.[8]

Death is ugly?
Oh, my children,
No.
If you knew
The beauty
That begins where
Your sight fails,
You would run,
Run, run
And leap
with open arms

---

[7] Lead Kindly Light, *Hymns*, 1985, #97.
[8] Carol Lynn Pearson, *Beginnings*, p. 61.

Into eternity . . .
I merely gave
Death
An ugly mask.[9]

## Enduring to the End

I once wondered why President J. Reuben Clark used to pray, fervently pleading that he could endure faithfully to the end. It seemed that a man of such stature before man and the Lord, had earned his crown. How cunning the adversary! How well he knows that if we let one foot to slip he may yet grasp us with his everlasting chains. Well did the Lord counsel when he said to Ezekiel that "when a righteous man doth turn from his righteousness, and commit iniquity . . . and shall die in his sin, . . . his righteousness which he hath done shall not be remembered."[10] Wherefore, "be ye clean that bear the vessels of the Lord,"[11] be believing, steadfast—a man for all seasons.

> *Behold, the Lord requireth the heart and a willing mind; and the willing and obedient shall eat the good of the land of Zion in these last days.*[12]

Having then obtained the fullness of the earth, the redeemed may look forward to the coming of the Bridegroom and the promised invitation to the marriage feast.

> *In the 22nd chapter of Matthew's account of the Messiah, we find the kingdom of heaven likened unto a king who made a marriage for his son. That this son was the Messiah will not be disputed, since it was the kingdom of heaven that was represented in the parable; and that the Saints, or those who are found faithful to the Lord, are the individuals who will be found worthy to inherit a seat at the marriage supper,*

---

[9] Carol Lynn Pearson, *Beginnings,* p. 56.
[10] Ezekiel 3:20.
[11] D&C 38:42.
[12] D&C 64:34.

*is evident from the sayings of John in the Revelation where he represents the sound which he heard in heaven to be like a great multitude, or like the voice of mighty thunderings, saying, the Lord God Omnipotent reigneth. Let us be glad and rejoice, and give honor to Him; for the marriage of the Lamb is come, and His wife hath made herself ready. And to her was granted that she should be arrayed in fine linen, clean and white: For the fine linen is the righteousness of Saints.*

*That those who keep the commandments of the Lord and walk in His statutes to the end, are the only individuals permitted to sit at this glorious feast, is evident from the following items in Paul's last letter to Timothy, which was written just previous to his death,—he says, "I have fought a good fight, I have finished my course, I have kept the faith: henceforth there is laid up for me a crown of righteousness, which the Lord, the righteous judge, shall give me at that day: and not to me only, but unto all them also that love His appearing."*[13]

"... He did not embrace the faith for honor in this life, nor for the gain of earthly goods. What, then, could have induced him to undergo all this toil?" We understand that Paul rested his hope in Christ, because he had kept the faith. For "if the Saints are not to reign, for what purpose are they crowned?" it was, as he said, that he might obtain the crown of righteousness from the hand of God.[14]

*There is to be a day when all will be judged of their works, and rewarded according to the same; that those who have kept the faith will be crowned with a crown of righteousness; be clothed in white raiment; be admitted to the marriage feast; be free from every affliction and reign with Christ on the earth, where,*

[13] *Teachings of the Prophet Joseph Smith*, p. 63.
[14] *Teachings of the Prophet Joseph Smith*, p. 64.

*according to the ancient promise, they will partake of
the fruit of the vine now in the glorious kingdom with
Him.[15]*

*And what shall others receive who do not labor
faithfully, and continue to the end? We leave such to
search out their own promises if any they have; and if
they have any they are welcome to them.[16]*

## A Summing Up

Your crown cannot be claimed in a single effort. But with faith in Him
you can prevail. So long as there burns one spark within your breast, you
can know that He still strives with you, anxious to have you look unto Him
in every thought and doubt not. There are sufficient places of glory in the
Kingdom of our God that each who will hearken to the counsel of the Lord
and to His servants will find a mansion prepared for him.

As control is gained over the appetites and passions of the natural
man, marvelous spiritual experiences follow. And as the Nephites of old,
one will "wax stronger and stronger in . . . humility, and firmer and firmer
in the faith of Christ, unto the filling [of one's soul] with joy and
consolation, . . . even to the purifying and the sanctification of [one's
heart], which sanctification cometh because of . . . yielding [to Christ]."[17]
It is having a perfect faith in the Holy One of Israel.

Then, as a trumpet giving a sure sound, you may go forth among those
of this generation inspired from on high and, by your witness, bring many
souls unto Christ. For after having feasted upon the words of Christ and
partaken of His redeeming power, you will desire with all your heart that
others might partake also. And this that they may be filled with hope and
joy like unto yourself.

By pressing consistently forward, in the day of the Lord, you may lay
claim upon your crown and shall thereafter receive all that the Father hath.

---

[15] *Teachings of the Prophet Joseph Smith*, p. 66.
[16] *Teachings of the Prophet Joseph Smith*, p. 64.
[17] Helaman 3:35.

All this is yours eternally as a joint-heir with Jesus Christ.

Now, lest the adversary prevail in teaching you his lies, find comfort and courage in the great testimony of Nephi.[18] He knew full well that we are subject to the laws of the flesh and to the law of the opposites until we have finished our sojourn here in mortality. He took no glory in his weaknesses, but rather desired to rejoice in Christ, the one in whom he had trusted.

The dynamic power of the Spirit of the Lord in man lies in the vision which he obtains. For knowledge will He, the Lord, send down out of heaven that ye might not walk in darkness, but in light.

Oh, be faithful to your covenants. For the ultimate crown is claimed only through the blessings and promises of the patriarchal priesthood. Remember that when the crown is placed upon your head it will only be when both you and your companion have jointly obtained eternal life. As you struggle together, all things necessary for purification will be made known. Pray always, and faint not; perform not anything unto the Lord, "save in the first place ye shall pray unto the Father in the name of Christ, that he will consecrate thy performance unto thee, that thy performance may be for the welfare of thy soul."[19]

> God hath not promised
> Skies always blue,
> Flower-strewn pathways
> All our lives through.
> God hath not promised
> Sun without rain,
> Joy without Sorrow,
> Peace without pain.
>
> But God hath promised
> Strength for the day
> Rest for the labor,
> Light for the way,

---

[18] See 2 Nephi 4:16-35.
[19] 2 Nephi 32:9.

Grace for the trials,
Help from above,
Unfailing sympathy,
Undying love.

—Anonymous

Wherefore, gird up your loins, fresh courage take. Put forth all the energy of your soul in building up the Kingdom of God on the earth and establishing a people who are pure in heart—even Zion. May it be said of you, "Well, done, thou good and faithful servant: thou hast been faithful over a few things, I will make thee ruler over many things."[20]

Know in your heart that there is nothing that can keep you from effecting the changes needed in your life and ultimately receiving the promise of all these blessings and glory. You can become perfect.

---

[20] Matthew 25:21.